Who Am I?

TRILLIONAIRES SAGA

Attain and Maximize Your Trillions

Dare Adebiyi

Dare's Group
Texas

Other Books also by **Dare Adebiyi**

The Series 1 & 2 of this Book:

1. Who Am I? Going Rogue: Discover and Become the Best You!

2. Who Am I? Big Dreams: Never Say Never About Your Dreams and Ambitions!

This is dedicated to the first set of Trillionaires the world is about to experience, of which I am one. And of course, those that will follow in our footsteps - the next set of Trillionaires. And, no, I did not forget you, to everyone we will be helping with our trillions.

Contents

We're Going Nuclear, Baby!
The 'Pride' that comes from Becoming Nuclear Aggression
or Defense Capable
Scary to know Mankind's Future-Today was Accurately
Predicted Millenniums Ago

Introduction

Starting From the Top

Hi there, how would you like to become a
Trillionaire? Yes, you read that correctly - not a
billionaire, but a Trillionaire? Impossible! I hear you
say. There currently is not one single Trillionaire alive,
and that is because there has never been anybody that
has ever become a Trillionaire! And there never will be
Trillionaire's, you say? Well, you are wrong! Because
there has been one Trillionaire in my dynasty several
hundred years ago; and the One who made him a
Trillionaire also promised the same for me - and you -
if you'll accept it!

My name is Zaphenath-Paneah - yeah, I know that's a
difficult name to pronounce or memorize - but I'm

sure you would quickly learn it because I am the second most powerful man in the whole world and you would definitely need my products, services or favor at one point or the other soon! Well, for those of you that still are biting your tongues in order to pronounce my name, I'll make it simple for you, just call me Joe Jake – my name before I suddenly became the second richest man alive!

And to make it even simpler, I am Joseph, the son of Jacob, from the B.C. era or time; and we are talking about my story today in the 21st century – isn't that cool? Do get the two prior books that acquaint you about my earlier years before I became the second most powerful man alive. They are:

1. Who Am I? Going Rogue - Discover and Become the Best You!
2. Who Am I? Big Dreams - Never Say Never About Your Dreams and Ambitions!

It feels great to introduce myself to you as the second richest and most powerful person alive, as I am sure you would gladly do the same if you were in my shoes. I'm also sure everyone would like to start at or from the top - from a vantage point; going into a challenge or competition that you know has already been decided for you to win; bidding for the contract you know has been decided for you to win because of insider information; having several nations depending on you for their food or safety; having the money that can buy other nations etc. – a position in which you are most likely to win a race, competition, deal or generally anything else in life?

I was born with a diamond spoon in my mouth – at the height of my dad's business and family success – when money and everything needed to make my growing up the envy of those who even considered themselves the crème de la crème of our nation's richest, were readily available. Yet, that birth status of mine is minor league compared to the major world league I am now a leader in. Now, I have unlimited uranium 235, 238, 239 and plutonium 239 spoons in my mouth – ensuring safety from every external national aggressions – as well as food and water supply spoons that can feed the whole world for almost a decade; all on my new adult birthday.

For those who do not know, those chemicals listed above are the primary ingredients for making atomic and hydrogen bombs; that the world's leading super power nations put together, already have the supply that can destroy the whole world a few times over. Many other nations however are also struggling to lay their hands on those materials to make such bombs too. Now, imagine this: Only two base models of such atomic bombs ended World War II in 1945, and led to the race for more sophistication and numbers of such weaponry all over the world.

Also, according to the World Health Organization, though the whole earth is covered by 71% water, only 2.5% of that water is fresh (drinkable) and only 1% is actually readily accessible. Also, more than 2 billion of the world's population do not have access to clean drinking water and by the year 2025, half of the world's population will be living in water-stressed areas. Drinkable water on its own is predicated to be a big enough reason for the start of a Third World War (WW III); without even touching on the shortage of food.

I'm sure the world's leading super power nations would quickly try to check the validity of my statement above on my endless supply of uranium - but you don't need to put yourself through all that trouble, you just need to read to the end of this book to validate that - Enjoy the read!

Chapter 1

Started at (or Reached) The Top? Yeah! Twice!!

Second Time the 'Charm'?

We all want to start at or reach the top of things in life because that almost guarantees success and protects against failure. Nobody likes to fail or be associated with failure because failure is associated with being at the very bottom of things – work, business, relationships, health, wealth, competitions and games. Success is what we want to be known for because it is synonymous with being at the top.

As a matter of fact, most people are willing to do just about anything in order to be successful and to avoid failure. We easily tell ourselves that 'I'll do it if the price is right'. If doing that 'thing' will ensure that I'll get that promotion, that raise, that contract, that guy, that girl, that championship gold, or whatever 'success' is to you; then I don't mind doing it!

I am sure you wouldn't mind going against the fastest man alive in a 100 meters race if you were given a head start of 99 meters, as well as a 9 second start ahead; which almost guarantees that you will win that race even if you were branded as a slow person in life.

How about getting in a boxing ring with Floyd Mayweather for a boxing championship bout, however only when he has just gone through about ten (10), fifteen (15) rounds championship bouts (without a break), with 10 of the biggest champions in the world; I am sure he would barely be able to stand and you would knock him out with just one soft punch of yours. Many boxers, and people would love to knock out Floyd 'the money', but alas, to no success.

I, Joe Jake, has had that privilege of starting from or reaching the top, twice (well, maybe more) in my life. You can get the nitty-gritty details on that from the 2nd book of the Who Am I? Series; namely: Who Am I? Big Dreams – Never Say Never About Your Dreams and Ambitions. I will however refresh our memories a little bit on it here for those who have not read the first volume. This however will only be a quick introduction on how I had started from the top at two different times during my life.

Caution: Everything at the Top Started from the Bottom

Before we go down memory lane on my starting at the top, let me throw you this word of caution though – Everything you will ever see at the top actually started at the bottom. Everything great starts small, and that's why God encourages us to 'not despise the days of small beginnings '; 'though your beginnings were small, your tomorrow or later days will be great or greatly increased'.

I actually didn't start at or from the top at those different times of my life but from the very bottom. Even before I was born, my parents tried to have a baby for so many years to no success; such that everyone soon labelled my mom as 'barren' or 'unfruitful'. This was even more painful and shameful because my dad had three more wives and all of them were having babies for him except my mom.

And when everyone had given up on my ever being conceived or born, God started out my life in a very small way in my mother's womb. I started out like a tiny dot on an expansive drawing canvas before God took me to the top at different times of my life. Even the Son of God was introduced into the world as a baby, but sacrificed Himself as a grown man.

When I was born, I immediately shot to the limelight and the forefront of everything about my family of origin. People around us couldn't ever get tired of hearing about me - the miracle child - the child no one ever though would make it into this world. And my older sibling soon got tired of 'this little boy' that was always 'stealing' their limelight and fame during every conversation.

Then they all collaborated, teamed up and formed an unholy alliance to 'get rid of me - the problem'. Their joint efforts soon led to my spiraling uncontrollably 'down to the bottom of life', like a tiny 'insignificant' speck of life. From being the talk of my large family and environment, I had been snuffed into 'nothingness' in a jiffy.

My ten half-brothers worked so well together to get rid of me and lied about it for almost two decades to our dad, that I never could stop wondering in my mind about the greatness that would have come out of their synergy, if only it had been surrendered to the leadership of the Almighty God; as opposed to them acting as their own 'God' or boss.

Before I also became the Chief of slaves or Managing Director of slaves - a type of being at the top - I was sold into slavery for years by my very own older siblings and countrymen. I was introduced into the nation of Egypt and the 'ownership' of General Potiphar as a slave. Again, the Most High did not forget me as He once again came through to lift me up after a while.

And, yes, before I became the Prime Minister of Egypt, I was lied against by my 'masters' wife, and was thrown into the dungeon (maximum security jail) for several years for a crime I never committed. Human beings love to be unfair, wicked and evil while they blame God for 'life being unfair and hard or evil'.

I found out time and time again that some who profess to love you are the very ones who will turn around and stab you in the back, push you down and stomp on you and your dreams, just so that they can get ahead of you. Without God, I would never have made it out of the pitfalls and dungeons of life that the 'closest' people around me threw me into, time and time again.

Down Memory Lane

My dad, Jake (Jacob), had gone through several decades of a very grueling season of growing his business and family under the 'tutelage' or 'mentorship' of his own uncle and father-in-law - my very own maternal grandpa Laban. My dad had earlier ran away from his own twin brother, my uncle Esau, whom he had conned or cheated a few times out of the most important things in our dynasty - the firstborn rights and the final fathers blessings reserved for only the first born son.

So, my dad ran far away to stay with uncle Laban in Paddan-Aram, where he had met my later to be mom, who happened to be the 'beautiful' one among the two daughters of uncle Laban. It was 'love at first sight' for my dad as he laid eyes on this astonishingly beautiful woman called Rachel. But dad was reportedly bankrupt and penniless at the time and so he struck a deal with his uncle to work for him for seven years without pay to serve as the payment for the necessary bride price to marry my mom to be.

Funny thing is that my dad had thought he was the best at deception, until his uncle and father-in law to be, switched the older, supposedly 'ugly' daughter, Leah in place of the younger daughter, Rachel, during the wedding ceremony. Novice dad was not aware of the swap until after the consummation of the marriage on the wedding night and the break of day the next day.

A quick word of advice here for married couples that believe in the 'silent' and 'no-lights on' or 'only extremely dimmed lights' for their bedroom life; I hope you don't have to find out the hard way later that someone else has been occasionally or regularly switched on you in the place of your husband or wife!

Don't 'enable' deception in your matrimonial room. Be like the first couple (Adam and Eve – before they rebelled against God) who were not ashamed of each other and 'kept full lights on' in their bedroom. Always remind each other that you and your spouse are fearfully and wonderfully made even into your oldest years.

Neither be a mute in your matrimonial bedroom, but turn out to be the loudest person in your neighborhood or anywhere else once outside your bedroom! Let everyone that has the breath of life, praise the Lord or make joyful noises with their own spouse in their matrimonial bedrooms – of course without being too loud that the rest of the people in their house and neighborhood get disturbed with your shouts of 'Hallelujah'.

That, however, served only as the beginning of the pains my dad started reaping for what he had sowed in deceiving his own dad and twin brother, decades earlier. Dad's own father-in law however continued to conn him out of his wages in order to keep him as a pauper, beggar and indirect slave for the rest of his life.

When dad eventually got restless, and tired of the poverty and servitude, he broke it off with the help of the Almighty God, and escaped away from grandpa Laban's siege that had been placed on his progress, success and prosperity. Another painful harvest during those years of drudgery, poverty and indirect enslavement, was that my dad's favorite wife among his now four wives - and my mom to be, Rachel - was never able to give birth to a single child; while the other wives were birthing out new babies regularly.

By the time my mom however gave birth to me, my father had finally broken off the indirect enslavement and poverty over his life, family and business. While all my older half-brothers were all born early to my dad and his other wives, they all had to grow up in indirect enslavement and abject poverty. And though my being born seemed to have been so long delayed for a few decades, I was however born at the height of my dad's prosperity - with a 'diamond' spoon in my mouth. You could thus say that I started from the top as a new born baby because it was at the period that my dad had experienced independence and fantastic financial success.

I had the time of my life growing up in unprecedented wealth, with practically everyone at my beck and call, until, out of envy and jealousy, my much older half-brothers decide to sell me off into slavery without the knowledge of our parents. I had fallen from the top and coveted diamond-spooned growing up position, down into the dungeons of enslavement. As if that was not enough, after several years of enslavement, I was also lied on to be a rapist, and so went even lower in life to an actual physical dungeon in the far away foreign nation called Egypt - the super power nation of the world.

But I thank the Most High God who did not leave me to rot there forever. In the most profound way, I was eventually pulled out of the dungeon by the most powerful king on earth, the Pharaoh of Egypt. I was made the official ruler of the nation, Egypt, with the king only considered higher than me ceremonially. And that was me starting again at the top again, only that this time around was unbelievably bigger than the earlier times – I was practically the richest and most revered man on the surface of the earth.

Actually, Maybe the Fourth Time was the 'Charm' for me!

Between those earlier 'starting at the top' extremes of my life however, there were two other times I seemed to have been promoted to the top. Both times just were not the type of 'top' positions that you would wish for anyone in life; but I did still appreciate both times. I was promoted to become the top slave in the house of General Potiphar – the end purchaser and user of the slave trafficking in which I was sold.

Even though I had become the 'Managing Director' of the slaves in his house, that promotion still did not earn me my freedom – the most basic right of every human being born into the world. Then after some time of being the top slave in my task masters house, his precious and 'innocent' wife decided she also had to 'have' me in her quest for 'fun' or extramarital affairs – cheating on her husband with me.

After I repeatedly declined her flirtatious 'friendship' that gradually turned to outright demands to sleep with her, she lied against me that I had tried to rape her, and I was quickly dethroned from my 'coveted' top slave position, and thrown into the dungeons of the king. Again, after some time in the dungeon, the Lord smiled on me as I was catapulted to the 'top' as the unofficial Prison Warden. Of course this top position was unofficial and also lacked the basest of human rights - freedom from slavery.

I pray for you that you will not give in to trap 'friendships' that are orchestrated to truncate your rise to the top of your life, game, studies, career, family, business and industry in Jesus name. I also declare that you will rise out of the dungeons of life to sit on the throne that the Most High already made ahead for you in Jesus mighty name.

It did seem as if that freedom from slavery or from being in the dungeons of life would never come for me, as the days turned into weeks and months and then years. But please be encouraged that the One Who put great dreams and ambitions into you, is faithful and dependable, and He will fulfill and actualize them eventually. But we must be patient and allow Him to work it all out in the best way that will ensure our lasting success, joy, freedom and productivity.

Whether it will be the second, third or fourth time that will do it for you, I decree that all that is necessary to catapult you to the top legally and not to anyone's detriment, will work in your favor in Jesus name. Dare to believe God and so do what is fair to others that you meet along your way of dream fulfillment, even if everyone else seem to be doing the opposite and cutting corners.

Chapter 2

Top Dog, Corner Office

Starting Out as a Billionaire

The Most High had pulled me out of the 'belly' of the earth and given me a seat higher than the biggest names on earth at the time. A seat above the most feared and revered among men – the Generals of the Great 'God'– the Pharaoh of Egypt. Men like General Potiphar, a millionaire who could 'buy' and 'own' exotic people of all color and creed, shipped from all over the world, as his 'properties' or slaves; and could do with them as he or his household pleased – like throwing the 'property' below the earth in a dungeon and forgetting 'it' ever existed.

I now sat as the official ruler of the most wealthy and technologically advanced nation of all, Egypt. And when you have the wealthiest people on earth at your beck and call, you automatically become a billionaire. Literarily from the dungeons to the Palace; from having absolutely no money or belonging, to owning the wealth of the super power of the world; from the unlikelihood of ever getting married, to marrying the most beautiful and prestigious lady on earth that other millionaires and rulers had been eyeing to marry for years –until I dashed their hopes by marrying her off the spinster roster of the world.

Here was I wearing the most expensive ring in the world ('A*b*amantium' alloyed with 'Vi*d*ranuim' and the 70 carat Oppenheimer Blue diamond stone worth $500 million), and singularly crafted for the Pharaoh of Egypt as his signature ring - only one of a kind. Of course, the king took it off his finger and put it on mine freely of his own volition, though I know the Lord was behind his doing so. But the king also gave me the ring with the 59.6 carat Pink Star diamond on 'A*b*amantium' worth $150 million to give to the wife he had also blessed me with as a wedding ring.

The Pharaoh also gifted me my custom made official 'Egyptllac' cars:

1. The only Zaphenath-Paneah (Z-P) Editions of the Maybach Exelero;

2. The only Joe Jake (J-J) Edition of The Rolls Royce Phantom Serenity;
3. Evening or leisure twin rides of the Bugatti Veyron and Chiron;
4. The Lamborghini Veneno; and
5. The Koenigsegg CCXR Trevita.

These rides made even leaders of other nations to drool whenever they visited Egypt land. Those were however just the beginnings of God restoring all my lost years of blessings; as we will see Him do even more later on.

The blessings and promotions I was experiencing were nothing short of what can only be called 'growing in grace and favor with God and men'. Ours was the wedding of the century that the Pharaoh threw for my wife and I. How else could I have afforded such a luxurious wedding since I had gone to sleep the previous night without a dime or any form of money in my pocket or to my name; and had been woken up in the early hours before daybreak to become practically the second richest man alive.. We were to live in the palace while our state of the art mansion right next to the palace was built over the next full year. You could definitely say about me that 'I had become the Top Dog with the Corner Office'.

What an awesome God the Most High is! Submit yourself under the mighty Hand of God, and He will lift you up in His own way and time is a very true and dependable saying – I know because I believed it, was guided and encouraged by it during the most challenging years of my life, and literarily saw it fulfilled in my very own life. I pray the good Lord will do the same for you and go beyond your wildest dreams in Jesus name.

It is not just individuals that want to start at or be at the top of things or top of their games in life, but groups, clubs, departments, companies and even nations are not left out of this deep seated desire. Everyone want to be the boss and have nobody to tell them what to do. At the heart of this deep seated desire, is the chaotic fact that people, groups, organizations and nations seem also unperturbed or care-less for whatever they have to do to be at the top.

The Master of Coup D'état's

The angelic leader, Lucifer was willing to orchestrate a coup d'état by leading one third of the angelic group to overthrow his and their creator, but failed miserably and became the fallen angel now called the devil. The devil has since then been in the business of deceiving others to follow in his failed footsteps of trying to be at the very top, at any deadly cost - of course to others.

So, the first couple also followed the Devil's lead and tried to get rid of God from their lives, only to find out that they had been tricked into handing their lives over to an evil genius. The first son of the first couple then went on to kill his younger brother because he wanted to feel ahead of him in the 'accepted offering to God realm'. And such evil has been the trend and norm ever since then.

Needless to say it, but that trickster Devil shot several wicked and evil thoughts into my heart as I had suddenly become so elevated beyond my wildest dreams and ambitions. The dreams and ambitions that had passed through my subconscious decades earlier on, were to be rise to the top in my family; but God has blown that right out of the water by taking me to the top of the world superpower nation.

But, just like the cunning serpent (the Devil) had deceived the first couple into believing that they had it good then, but could have it best if they chose to rebel against the authority and claim of their Creator over them, and to become their own personal 'Gods'; He strongly suggested to my heart to rebel against the Pharaoh. He suggested I should oust the Pharaoh, and then become the 'most powerful' man on earth. He said being the number 2 man in the world could never be good enough, and this calls for a coup d'état.

I however consciously and continuously surrendered my mind and thoughts under the covering of the Most High God for safe keeping and victory over such evil thoughts and suggestions such as those that came on planning the violent overthrow and demise of the Pharaoh. I chose to count my blessings and name them one by one to express utmost gratitude to God and deep appreciation to the people He has used to bless me.

The Devil is indeed very wicked for him to have suggested to my heart to overthrow the very one person whom the Almighty had used to favor and promote me to unimaginable heights of success in my career, health, wealth, family and status. How the devil likes to use us to destroy one another in life, especially in the unnecessary pursuit of becoming the 'top dog'. He wanted me to kill the Pharaoh, all his family, and all those loyal to him.

When those evil thoughts didn't 'see the light of day' in me, I thought that battle was over – boy, was I wrong. I soon found out that the Devil is one of the most persistent and ingenious personalities ever, as he will not give up without a decisive fight and not until he has utilized every avenue and innovation possible to get his goals achieved. He will keep coming back with 'better offers' and through other people and avenues that you would least expect to have to refuse their 'generous offers'.

Hardly had I become the Pharaoh's right hand man and the number two most powerful man in the world, than I soon started getting offers from people in and outside the Pharaoh's 'trusted' circle of Generals, friends and even family members, to help me 'get to the very top'; of course by helping me take down the Pharaoh. They said that the Pharaoh had had his time of ruling, but that 'this was my time'; after all, 'you are the only man who the gods used to solve the Pharaoh's unsettling nightmares and definitely the very best among mankind'. Betrayal is one of the Devil's most tactful weapons that seems to get the job done for him.

Once he promises people 'great' rewards of promotions, money, fame, status, worship from others, or even just the 'satisfaction' of revenge; he has seen one too many people who never fail to pass up on such lucrative 'once in a lifetime' opportunities. My ten half-brothers didn't pass upon their opportunity to become rich in selling me into slavery; and Judas Iscariot also made sure he bit the opportunity to become rich in selling out Jesus.

What 'great' opportunities of 'becoming' rich or successful are you biting today by betraying those closest to you or who have even put their lives on the line for you at one point or the other? Do you really think such evil and wicked thoughts (even suggestions from other 'well-meaning' people) going through your mind are originally yours, or they are sneaked in by a deceiving wicked personality called the devil?

Let me break it down to you as simple as possible – you do not stand a chance of winning against the 'opportunities' and baits of the Master Deceiver without a higher help, without the Help of the Most High God. Learn from the victims of such duels with the Devil over time. The only ones that bested him had the Help of the Creator, the Most High God. And I gladly received that help of the Most High in order to be able to 'pass over' such 'upward calls to greatness'.

The Devil also suggested that since the 'tables of power had now turned in my favor', one of the things I should also make a priority was to avenge myself on all those who had done me wrong at different times. He shot wicked thoughts into my mind to go after General Potiphar and his wife to make sure they suffered tremendous public disgrace and pain for living against me and shutting me up in the 'bowels of the earth' for years.

He also suggested to take a long trip back to my homeland and family of origin with a great army at my command so as to go and punish my ten half-brothers who had sold me into slavery a few decades earlier. He gave me thoughts and visions of being able to derive satisfaction from watching all those who had been wicked to me suffer greatly at 'my mighty hands'. After all, my hands were obviously now 'mighty'.

I however drew from the strength of the Most High in prayers, worship and surrender, and actively refused to continue to entertain such thoughts. This is because God had commanded that 'vengeance belonged to Him alone, and He will repay each person for the choices that they make against others, in His own way and time'. And anyone who also wants to usurp that authority of God on vengeance will only find themselves also at the receiving end of God's anger for attempting to share in His glory and for getting in His way while He is bringing judgement on the guilty.

Success and power can prove too strong to handle for a heart that is not submitted to the Almighty God. A heart that does not consciously stay under God, will easily be 'hacked' or remotely taken over by the deceiving Devil. And once he gains a little access to such hearts and minds, he forcefully takes it over and controls it to carry out unimaginable acts of wickedness against others.

Chapter 3

Nuclear Capable - Top of the Food Chain

We're Going Nuclear, Baby!

The nuclear power armament became the biggest 'getting to the top' priority for the human race after just two of the basest models of the first set of nuclear bombs led to the abrupt end of World War II and the unequivocal surrender of one side to the other. After several years of a global war that did not seem to have had a decisive end in sight and after several years of it being waged with the highest number of human casualties - military and civilian - in the history of the world; the atomic or nuclear bombs seemed to have been the 'answer'.

Not only did the nuclear bombs stop World War II (WW II) – which started barely twenty years after the end of World War I (WW I) – but it seems to have prevented the start of World War III for currently more than 70 years after WW II ended. The devastation that those 2 nuclear bombs achieved were so great – wiping out 2 cities – that no country has ever launched any of such weapons of mass destruction (WMD) ever since; even though more sophisticated and deadlier weapons – hydrogen and disease spreading bombs – than those initial ones have been created in several super power nations as of date.

So, after the first and the second attempts at world peace for the human race, can we safely say the second time was the charm – that achieved lasting world peace – or we seem closer to the third and potentially the world-devastating attempt ever? The US and Russia (formerly Soviet Union) emerged as the predominant world super powers from WW II and started the Cold War of Nuclear Armament to the extent that the stock pile and sophistication of the bombs each of these two countries have, can not only destroy each other's nations several times over, but actually destroy the whole world a few times over too. Yet there are several other nations of the world who have also already attained this 'prestigious' rank and file of a nuclear power nation or state.

It seems there is more to the 'continuous tuning' and stock piling of nuclear and biological WMD's other than a deterrent to external aggressions from other capable countries though. There seems to be great preparation for deterring 'other than this world' external aggression of 'other's out there - gods or aliens with super powers' - like Nick Fury put it in the *fictional movie* 'Avengers (2012)', when he referred to Thor (the god of thunder) as such when he suddenly showed up on earth and became a threat from 'another world'.

Or, like the Batman came to the conclusion that the 'god' (Superman) - 'an alien from another planet', who had metamorphosed into 'god' (alien with super powers) on earth, and whose presence on earth had attracted other 'gods' to come to earth looking to kill him in the movie 'Man of Steel' (2013), and 'Batman v Superman: Dawn of Justice' (2017). Superman's battles soon led to countless loss of lives and properties, which quickly defined him as 'too big a threat to the existence of the human race' and should be killed by a capable human like himself.

Or, in the *fictional movie* 'Rapture - Palooza (2013)' where a guy was able to shoot dead, 'Jesus', who appeared in the sky on a white horse for the end-time battle of the world. He had shot 'Jesus' with a laser canon which might indirectly depict nuclear capabilities meant to fight and 'kill' the alien 'God' whenever He shows up to reclaim the world He claims to have created and own.

It becomes probable that the nuclear armament that is able to destroy the whole world a few times over does have a target bigger that the world, probably the God who claims to have created all people and things and also claims to have sacrificed His Son for the 'salvation' of mankind from the control and enslavement of the ancient dragon and deceiver called the devil. The God Who has promised that everyone who takes or accepts the salvation His Son purchased from the devil through His own death and resurrection, would escape the forever punishment He will bring on the devil and those that follow him to do evil and wickedness.

Man had bitten and continues to bite the fruit of seeking complete independence from his Maker right from the first man and woman. Even though God gave the first couple immense independence over the earth with a free will, the deceiver made them to believe it never was good enough. So he was able to trick them into rebelling against God in order to trap them under him (the devil himself).

Even till this day, the greater percentage of the world appear to be enthusiastically biting the same fruit of seeking complete independence from God at all cost, and seem 'ready to defeat' God in the Third World War (WW III) that has been brewing for decades and likely to happen in the nearest future.

Every major nation in the world today however have made it a matter of national priority to become a nuclear-weapon State, or at the very least, have nuclear weapons to 'defend' itself against external aggression, or be regarded as nuclear aggression capable. So many nations will pay outrageous amounts of money to be able to boast of being in possession of nuclear weapons.

You should however not be surprised that it is not only sovereign states and nations that are seeking the 'power, control, prestige, and massive aggression capabilities' that nuclear weapons 'confer', but many individuals see it as a means of becoming very rich or a Trillionaire. Such individuals seek to either continuously trade in nuclear weapons, or to obtain them and threaten nations and states with such in order to obtain billions and trillions from them.

Becoming a Trillionaire is a 'top' position in life that many individuals consider to be their own personal race and destiny. And many really are unconcerned how they get to that top Trillionaire position, whether they have to bankrupt millions of other people through continuously staying a step ahead of laws and regulations on creating casino styled investment and retirement schemes that are made to look like they were created for the best interest of the investor, or enslaving others in so many others ways covered in book 2 of the Who Am I? Series; namely (Who Am I? Big Dreams – Never Say Never about Your Dreams and Ambitions); or becoming nuclear aggression capable.

The 'Pride' that comes from Becoming Nuclear Aggression or Defense Capable

There is a huge 'pride' that comes as a result of becoming nuclear or hydrogen bomb capable. It is a palpable pride that makes other nations very weary of getting on the 'bad' side of the capable nations. No nation wants literarily millions of their people and their cities wiped out as a result of nuclear and biological weapons of mass destruction (WMD) strikes.

And so the nations with great nuclear capabilities have become the top of the food chain and are thus feared and revered by other nations below them. It is however a true saying that pride goes before a fall as we have seen over the course of the existence of mankind how many nations that rise to the top, soon feel no need for God anymore. God suddenly seems to become a myth and playtime of the uneducated, undeveloped, poor and the mundane. He suddenly gets booted to the bottom just like the other conquered or less powerful nations quickly get booted to the bottom.

The conqueror nations soon believe that they have conquered God too and that they are no longer under Him. They soon get so irritated with the notion of God that they would do everything possible to wipe out His name or memories from 'their' great nation. Who needs a God when you have 'attained' the position of a 'god', and even sweeter still, when your nation and leaders have also become their own 'Gods?' And which national leaders would want a God that tells them not to do anything they fancy or that feels good to them; not to even talk about allowing their people to believe in such God rather than them?

Scary to Know Mankind's Future–Today Was Accurately Predicted Millenniums Ago

The most intriguing thing to note about the ongoing collective nuclear capabilities across the globe being able to destroy the world several times over, is the fact that God already said (predicted) more than 2,000 years ago in His written Word, the Bible, that once everyone that would accept the saving grace and way of escape from judgement on evil that His Son, Jesus, made available to *all* people, have done so, He would then remove such people to His Kingdom for a season.

That season is called the Marriage supper (ceremony) of the saved people to their Savior in God's kingdom; during which a concurrent season called the Tribulation (terrible times) would be taking place on earth. God will then destroy this present world and all the evil in it with fire, before making another new earth that has no room for evil or wickedness. And finally comes the eternal or forever bliss of the saved people, concurrent with the forever punishment of those that ignored God's forgiveness.

The reality is that human beings have actually created enough nuclear bombs to destroy the world several times over in *fire*, all in our quest to be at the 'top' without having to answer to anyone else, especially not the Almighty God. Man claims that God could not be a God of love if He will punish sin or evil and evil doers by destroying the evil saturated world; while it is mankind ourselves who have created enough firepower that will destroy the world – and we still are creating more.

Many people also claim to **not** have been created and will do everything possible to fight against the claim of the Almighty God over their 'right to freedom' to be their own personal 'God'. Most of mankind will do anything in order not to have to listen to a God who tells them to do what is good and right to other people just as we would want other people to do the same good and right things to us.

Many nation's leaders tout 'religious freedom' of not having to answer to any God, while they have hundreds of thousands of laws and rules that every human being that is a citizen of that country or that does business with them have to obey and follow, or else, they will be 'severely punished' or reprimanded. We consider it **wrong** for there to be a God Who hates and will punish wickedness, but consider it **alright** for mankind to punish wickedness perpetrated by other people.

Many countries drum 'freedom' into the ears and minds of children as soon as they start the earliest form of formal education, and tell them that they never even need to be under the authority of their biological parents or guardians. They tell the children that they should report their parents to the 'authorities' to be punished or put in check (locked up or jailed) if the parents were to discipline them or punish them for doing wrong things and breaking their household rules, while they expect such children to grow up and be under the authority of the nation and ***not*** break the laws of the nation.

Many nations and their law makers, interpreters and enforcers fail to properly define the 'freedom' they encourage to their citizens. Instead of properly defining it as 'freedom to do what is right and does not hurt others'; they rather define it as 'freedom to do anything you feel like doing at any time, to anyone without anybody being able to restrain you' – a very terrible error indeed.

Do companies succeed by teaching new employees not to have to follow the directions of their first line supervisors, and that they should report such supervisors to the 'management' if the supervisor enforces the rules of the company? How many companies succeed by telling their new hires that they were their own bosses and have the 'freedom' to do whatever they like; and also get the supervisor arrested and locked up if they try enforcing the company rules?

Is it then a surprise that many children grow up as a 'god' to themselves, without ever wanting to follow any parental rules or authority; and definitely not wanting to follow any rules or authority of the nation that had helped them to form the habit of not having to obey anybody over them *except* their own selves? That is why many children just want to do 'whatever' feels good to them – whether it is to curse others, 'roast' others (call others terrible names), bully others, take (steal) what is not theirs, shoot and kill anyone who doesn't want to allow them to take what they want, rape anyone who doesn't want to submit to their advances of 'love', and kill them if they resist, or just kill them for the fun of having raped and having the power to 'send them out of their misery'.

Chapter 4

Freedom Galore

I am Free to Do Anything I want! Really?

Nowadays, children do not want to follow directions from school teachers or even law enforcement agents like the police; all because they have been taught that nobody should have to tell them what to do. Children want to tell parents and teachers and the police 'what to do' as opposed to them first learning to respect and follow the first line of authority that they came through into the world – their parents - so as to get accustomed to following other proper authorities before becoming grown-ups and being able to write proper laws that help maintain peace and sanity in a nation and the world as a whole.

Many nations drum 'freedom' into the ears of their babies and children while they themselves have absolutely no clue what true freedom is, or Who Freedom is, or Who is truly able to give freedom. Or, maybe many nation's leadership just have erroneously chosen to rather buy a 'photocopy' or the fake of True Freedom, which is called a Lie, and which can only be bought from the greatest Liar, Deceiver and Trickster that ever lives – the Devil or the Father of Lies.

And because the leadership of many nations have bought the lie, from the 'Father of lies', they have also unwittingly indirectly submitted to the Liar's rulership, just like the first man and woman did in the garden of Eden. Such leaders are sadly selling Satan's lies to the next generation of children. The children are told that there is no God, and that they have freedom to be their own 'god', and to do whatever they like or feels good to them without a concern for how it affects anybody else. But of course, they are then expected to grow up and suddenly be able to submit to the rules and laws of the society they are part of – isn't that an irony?

The painful thing is that mankind was tricked into submitting to the leadership of the devil with the 'promise of freedom' from God's rules. Yet, most of mankind has however intentionally chosen to remain under the Deceiver's lies of 'freedom' because the lie just seems too good to resist. I mean, who doesn't want the 'freedom' of not having to answer to anybody or system or government or God? Who doesn't want to be able to do anything he or she wants without any repercussions or punishment from parents, teachers, faith leaders or government leaders?

Who wouldn't like to cheat, steal, lie or even kill in order to win competitions, contracts, economic and social positions of leadership, money and power? Who wouldn't want to rule the world and make everyone else a slave to himself or herself? Who wouldn't want to take all the riches and power in the world and become the 'most powerful man or woman in the world?' Who wouldn't want to do anything – and I mean 'anything' – to get to such positions in life? Sadly, most people will do just about anything – even the most unthinkable and unimaginable – to be 'at the top of the world'; *except one man.*

He Did It for You and Me!

That man was also given the same opportunity of not having to submit to any other authority 2,000 years ago by the Trickster and Deceiver himself, the old Dragon – the Devil. That man came to submit himself in the most justified way to lawfully, legally or rightly rescue mankind from under the lies, trickeries and enslavement of the Devil. That man came to pay the unattainable price needed to restore mankind back to the position of true, but gracious leadership over the world he was given to rule over after creation; which he inadvertently lost to the Trickster.

That man came to pay the debt that mankind could never pay, and would never still be able to pay if given forever to do it. That man came to live a righteous life (cleared by God and man as sinless – Pontus Pilate representing unbiased human government and leadership, declared him as sinless compared to the biased religious leaders of his day). Yet, he willingly surrendered to be brutalized and eventually killed in the most shameful, painful and public way to satisfy the debt of sin, rebellion, wickedness and every unimaginable evil thing that people do all over the world.

Man can never live righteously or in the right way while still under the trickeries of the Trickster, the Devil. And because of mankind's tainted or sinful nature, he does not qualify to offer himself as a sinless ransom or exchange to bear the punishment for sin and set the rest of mankind free. Man's tainted nature (selfish nature) would rather sacrifice other people for punishment than to sacrifice himself or herself for others.

This same God had also said more than 2,000 years ago in His Word that when the battle that will eventually destroy the world begins, there would be no place to hide. This was long before man got anywhere near creating satellites that are launched into space and can accurately pin-point the exact location of any human being on earth through GPS - Global Positioning System. The GPS is widely used to give locations and direct people from one place to another - whether it is on land, in the air or by the seas.

As of today, cell phones or mobile phones are in almost every home and adult's hands all over the world. As of March, 2013, the U.N. offered statistics from its recent study that showed that more people had access to mobile phones than to clean water or proper toilets (as opposed to open defecation that easily spreads diseases). But the children are not allowing themselves to be left behind in the quest to have a mobile phone too. Many children in several countries easily convince their parents of the necessity of their having a mobile phone just to 'stay in touch' with them and so that 'the parents or guardians can always easily reach them'.

As much as mobile phones have become the norm, wearables (smart watches and movement trackers) are even becoming more of the 'necessity'. Many smart wearable now have LTE connectivity and carry their distinct individual calling number just like the smart phones do. Mankind seems to have gotten to the stage of anyone on earth being able to reach any other person on earth by dialing or calling their individual watch or phone number. And any mobile phone or wearable (watch) is easily trackable anywhere in the world today.

Also, God said in His written Word over 2,000 years ago that man would have developed the individual numbering system for each individual for the end times when world leaders would stage the last coup d'état to rid the world of the people of the 'God' Who said everyone that accepts His free salvation from Satan's evil control become 'citizens' of Heaven – God's world that the greatest earthly scientific minds have searched tirelessly through space, trying to find.

World leaders consider such a place an alien world and are uncomfortable with the citizens (aliens or gods) of such place currently being human citizens in their nations now, but having the faith and 'alien' powers to be able to 'fly out' of this world to meet their Savior in the sky and then disappear for a long time (years), while their God rains down judgement on the remaining world that refused the claim of that God over them.

World leaders have searched and combed outer space for a long time trying to find this Heaven place that contains the spirits of departed people of God (a.k.a. aliens) and that some of their earthly citizens are predicted to likely be whisked away in the twinkling of an eye later at some point in time. But even more threatening is that several of the individuals who claim to be 'believers' in that God, but who choose to still be their own gods, would be left behind on earth in the first 'whisking away - rapture'; and they would want to refuse to submit to the World leaders demand to 'tag' everyone left with an allegiance and tracking numbering system, chip or implant (coded 666).

The world leadership at that time would have prepared to 'defend the earth and its people' from any 'supposed' punishment on evil and wickedness. Of course the world leadership at that time will be functioning under the direct full blown leadership of the evil and wicked deceiving Devil, who promises 'freedom' but indirectly rules and enslaves people to do evil to others and themselves eventually.

And so, the world leaders would want to torture the left behind 'believers' (who were church goers who had operated under the lies of the devil that they could profess to belong to God while living in disobedience to Him), in order to get accurate location information on 'where' their God is 'hiding' and operating from as He sends judgement on the earth.

Such believers would eventually be killed because they cannot tell the 'whereabouts' of God, His people and their Kingdom. The world leadership will also be very frustrated and brutal in unimaginable ways because their GPS systems and satellites cannot find God. The Jewish people will also be a prime target of the world leaders, because the Savior that God sent into the world to rescue mankind from evil, in the person of Jesus Christ, thousands of years ago, was from the Jewish nation.

The world would insist that they do not, and would never need a savior because they are doing just fine and enjoying their 'fun' (wicked and evil) lifestyles. They would demand to know from the Jewish people and believers, where this God is because they have some nuclear and hydrogen bomb 'presents for Him that they want to come and lay at His feet 'in worship' and see if He can still stand or lay claim to the world after they are detonated.

Most nations have individual identifying numbers for each person that is a citizen, visitor or an alien/foreigner (someone from another nation), such that every activity - trades, transactions, buying, selling, internet usage and location, programs watched and when - that they do is easily traceable to each person. Most nations will also argue that in order to prevent wicked attacks on their citizens, they would need to track, record and continuously analyze every activities of even their own citizens at all time.

Practically every device and gadgets everywhere are now connected to the internet and can be remotely 'hacked' or taken over by someone else who is on the other side of the nation or the world. Whether it is your phone, smart watch, TV, media player, smart thermostat, smart lock, smart key, smart car, traffic light cameras, house or neighborhood or workplace cameras, someone else quite far away can hack into it and take control of it.

Be wise today and put your faith in the God Who predicted mankind's future status of the pride of achieving 'independence' from Him, and because most developed nations are now at the 'top' of the food chain - which was where God originally put us before the deceiving Devil tricked us to 'work hard' to become 'self-sufficient and self-governing' so that we can be 'very proud of our hard worked achievements'. Escape the judgement that was originally meant for the Devil and other fallen angels that were swayed by him. Ask

Jesus to simply *save or remember* you in His Kingdom today.

Chapter 5

Successful Management or CEO Succession 101

Determining the Need for New Leadership, Management or CEO

'**U**neasy is the head that wears the crown' is a common saying that simply means that leadership is not an easy job or position. But I bet many will beg to differ because that saying is really applicable to only conscionable leadership - those that will lead with a good conscience to do what is right and beneficial for the good of the people they are leading as opposed to their personal selfish good.

It actually is a lot of 'fun' for selfish and wicked leaders to rule and reign because they will direct the resources meant to take care of all the people under them - group, workers, family, state, nation, region, or continent - to their personal gain and use alone; without an iota of care about what happens to the rest of the governed.

This is why the scriptures say that, 'the governed groan or cry when the wicked rule, but rejoice and are glad when the right-minded people rule'. This is because the natural state of the mind of mankind under sin and the trickster Devil is nothing short of wickedness. Or how else can you explain when leaders of nations wage unwarranted wars that costs their nations the lives of so many young soldiers and civilians (women and children inclusive), only for the leaders to lace their personal pockets or coffers with the spoils or gains of such wars?

Or when leaders make it their day to day job or effort to find out how they can spend or waste the revenue of a whole nation on their personal selves and those 'loyal' to them, while the rest of the governed people live 'from hand to mouth' in abject poverty and lack? Or how does a person sell the things that they know will lead to loss, heartaches, death and destruction of the users and those connected to them, when the seller and manufacturers tout their products as 'the best thing that can happen to you', or 'I'm making you rich', or 'I'm doing you a very big favor'?

A leadership that looks out for the good of the people it is leading is very uncommon and unnatural. Such leadership obviously is under the leadership of the Almighty God Whose most important directive is to 'do to other people, what you would want other people to do to you'. How many people would want their own children's brains to be fried by the hard drugs that they manufacture and sell to others?

How many would want to sell their own selves, or their daughters (or son's) into the Adult sex slavery business, or others forms of slavery? How many are willing to sacrifice themselves and their families in uncalled for wars? How many will sell guns to mentally disturbed young people who attend the same school as their own children, knowing that there is a possibility that such a person could go on a shooting spree and kill their own children in the bid?

The most important thing that determines that a group or people or company or nation is in need of new leadership is when the old leadership has decided through their actions and lifestyles that they do not need the oversight of their Creator, the Most High, anymore. When they or the people they are leading, in their 'wisdom' determine that they have all they need to lead themselves without anything to do with the Almighty.

A peoples actions will speak quite louder than their words if they reject the counsel, wisdom, leading and directives of the Almighty, and rather chose to go the opposite way. Just like king Saul was instructed to carry out God's judgement on a nation (Amalek), but he as well as the people he led chose to rather 'do their own thing' as opposed to following God's instructions. This immediately led to God changing the leadership of the nation when He asked the prophet Samuel to go and anoint the next king in the person of the young boy David.

It is noteworthy to know that change in leadership was set in motion in the unseen spiritual world by the Most High, but the process spanned about 2 decades to be fully completed in the physical world. Even when God had rejected Saul from being king, God was patient with him over a long period of time looking out for Saul to turn away from self-rule and doing whatever pleased him and the people around him. Saul however kept going further and further down the path of destruction as he progressed in doing the most unimaginable things.

How else could you explain how when God used a small boy in David to save all of Israel from impending slavery to the Philistines, since they couldn't find anyone willing to fight Goliath to the death for their freedom; that King Saul then determined that David's victory against Goliath had made him too famous for his own good, and it was best to kill him or hunt him down like a game?

King Saul who had also promised that whoever delivered his nation from the 'Goliath-fix' they found themselves in would also be given the hand of the Princess in marriage; soon quickly turned around into a father-in-law who spent the rest of his life and national leadership into hunting his son in law for the kill. When a person or group decides to turn their backs to God, they will likely realize too late later on that they have inadvertently turned to embrace the Devil, who is the master of wickedness.

If only Saul and his men had returned back to following God, they would have saved themselves and the whole nation they led from the death and destruction they soon brought on themselves from the Philistine nation. If only Saul had not pursued the only man that God had given unanimous victory over the Philistines, time and time again, in the person of David, they would as a nation not have fallen in tremendous losses to the Philistines in a later battle.

The case of King Saul's evils toward David was however much farther off in the future of Israel, as opposed to when the Pharaoh of Egypt - the king of a nation that wasn't familiar with the Most High God at the time – successfully determined that leadership succession had been put in motion by the Almighty God; yet, he was wise enough to submit to God and carry out such succession according to God's directives.

No wonder Jesus said that the first will be the last while the last will be the first. There are many peoples, leaders and nations that many others (supposedly connected to God), believe are very unfamiliar with the Almighty God, and are so not likely to follow His directives, who will show much more wisdom, humility and submission to God when they have an encounter with the Most High. They are the ones who will populate the Kingdom of God, which is built specifically for those that will submit to God's leadership and oversight – and yes, they will also choose to receive the mercy of God through the sacrifice of His son, Jesus.

Who are your Friends or Advisors?

It is one of the most amazing things to me that a supposed 'pagan' or 'unbelieving' or 'infidel' person, leader, or king like the Pharaoh of Egypt, could listen to God Almighty telling him that it was time for a new leadership; and for him to willingly submit to that directive of God to him through his dreams of the night. It deeply humbles me that the Pharaoh released all the authority and power he had wielded before to a 'nobody' like me - a nobody to those who chose not to listen to God, but a somebody to God and those who submit to Him. Yet, a supposedly believing, anointed and ordained king in the person of King Saul refused such simple transfer of authority decades later as if he had no precedence to learn from or refer to.

It is also very noteworthy that the people that the Pharaoh had surrounded himself with in leadership were in agreement with Him when He chose to listen to the directives of the Most High on the process to engage in, so as to save their nation from impending doom from the years of famine ahead. While, unfortunately, it was the people that surrounded King Saul in his failed leadership, that were the very ones who encouraged him to stage a coup against God to oust Him from leading them as a nation and group.

Whoever moves with the wise will become wiser, but the companion or friend of 'fools' will suffer many harms and destructions, is a true and dependable saying. It is also very true that it is the 'fool' that say's in his or her heart, that there is no God, and make themselves their own 'Gods'.

Who are the people you have surrounded yourself with in life? Are they people who do not want to acknowledge the oversight of God and want to just do whatever they feel like doing? Or are they people who even 'profess or confess to know' God on the outside in their actions and when around other 'religious' people, but in their hearts, they dismiss God and do whatever they like when among their true 'friends'?

This is also a pivotal place in many company's, conglomerate's, groups and nation's journey that many leader's hold on to the reins of leadership because 'they don't want to be regarded as ex-leaders, ex-champions, ex-governors, ex-senators, ex-CEO's, ex-presidents etc. Unfortunately, they do so to the detriment and unimaginable losses of the people they govern, but definitely also to their own eventual traumatic losses and demise.

As a CEO, CFO, COO, President, Manager, Supervisor, Senator, Governor or leader of any sort, be willing to face the reality that you would need to step down one day for God's chosen new leadership for your own sake and the good of the populace. Be like the Pharaoh who had initially started out as a 'god' to himself, but who was humble enough when it was time for him to recognize the presence of the Almighty God in his domain, and His directive for him to hand over the leadership of the nation to the one person whom He had prepared to lead and ensure successful continuity.

The Saul Mindset?

Do not be like King Saul who was supposed to be close to God but who allowed envy, jealousy, hatred, bad company and the love of money, power and fame to ruin him, his generations and the nation he was supposed to be leading. There are so many leaders of companies, ministries, groups and nations who overstay their leadership and do not even have any succession plans in place for any eventualities.

King Saul never submitted to the succession plan of God for the nation he was leading, but put his own succession plan in place for his own son to succeed him as the king of Israel. Unfortunately, king Saul and three of his son's (including the son he had prepped to take over from him) died on the same day in a battle that God already warned them would be fatal for them. He threw the lives of his future generations into the wind, such that even the other son's that were not killed in battle that day were eventually killed over the next few years under terrible circumstances.

Are you kicking against God's choices for the next leadership because they are not your own son's or descendants, or because you fear they may do a much better job than you and look better in achievements over time (or mess up all you have worked for); or you fear that they may also expose terrible things you have done over time as the leader, or you believe people who look different from you or are from a different background than yours are simply not meant to be in leadership, even if God has unequivocally chosen them and you know it?

Think about the losses your 'independence' from God would eventually cause you, the generations after you and the people you are leading, all because you have unknowingly or intentionally submitted yourself and the people you are leading to the one Deceiver spirit whose interest and expertise is simply 'to steal, kill and destroy' every good thing you hold dear to you.

Chapter 6

Successful Management or CEO Succession 201

Designated Successor or Survivor

Do you have a designated survivor(s) for the leadership position you occupy today, or will the people be thrown into chaos and confusion if any unexpected thing were to happen to you as their leader? Is the person(s) meant to succeed you well trained and empowered by you so that they can succeed without you in the eventuality of your expected or unexpected departure or demise?

Strategizing

Are the proposed strategies of your successor what you also buy into as capable of leading to continuous and future successes? Are there issues you may need to iron out with your likely successor that may jeopardize the business, group, state or national entity they may likely be leading after you? Is your successor fully informed on all he or she needs to know to be able to make the most educated decisions?

What were your own secrets of success that you believe are imperative for your successor to know so as to enhance his or her likelihood of success? Are you willing to have your successor succeed far above you or you are intent on sabotaging his or her success, so as to make yourself look more successful on the long run? The Pharaoh made sure I had access to him and his think-tank in order to become acquainted with the leadership task ahead.

Cultivating Necessary Traits

What are the traits in your designated survivor or successor that you have observed that would likely add to their chances of success or that may rather stunt, hinder or irreparably destroy all of the good work that has been achieved over a long time, and that is being passed down or handed over for continuity?

What are the traits you believe can and should be cultivated in the designated successor to ensure their success? The Pharaoh observed that I was not married because I had been a slave and later a prisoner for the last several years of my life, but since I had now become the de-facto ruler over Egypt, he said that I would need the best, most supportive and beautiful wife. He however didn't just observe and say it, but he went further in getting me such a wife; thus, he ensured the building of my family as a necessary stability trait.

Battles and Challenges

What are the battles or challenges you believe you need to win or take care of before the baton is passed-on to your successor, because you know that those are battles or challenges that you created, or that showed-up as a result of your unique personality; and that you are the one that should take care of it before handing over to the next generation?

Who or what are the sworn enemies that you need to handle as appropriately as possible to ensure they do not spring surprise attacks that your successor is unlikely going to be able to successfully respond to? Have you made the tools to successfully handle destabilizing forces – foreign and domestic – readily available to your successor?

Reparation or Restitution

What were your most undignified moments that you wish you had handled differently, and which you wish or want nobody to ever find out about – the errors and mistakes you had made during those uneventful times? The things you would almost give anything or do anything to make sure that they do not see the light of day? The reality is that there is almost nothing that you are not able to go back to, in order to revisit and make corrections and amends as much as possible and to your best capabilities. Your amends and corrections may definitely not completely redress the error or wrong, but your willingness to own up to the error and do everything you can to correct it is really what is needed and what truly counts.

Ally Buy-In

Who are the allies that have helped you to succeed during your times? They would likely be glad to extend the same help or courtesy to your successor as long as they know you have given your successor unequivocal approval, introductions and backings. Have you introduced your likely successor to the people who he or she can trust; and indirectly introduced him or her also to the people they need to be very wary of – careful around?

You have to be able to vouch for the successor when introducing him or her to those that will support them and help them to succeed, before such allies will also be able to trust them and commit to their person as well as the continuous goals of the group, company, venture, organization or nation.

And the same also goes for vouching for your allies to the successor to be, so that he or she also can safely know those who are for them and the group's vision or mission; as well as those who cannot be counted on or trusted.

Vet

Also ensure that your successor to be has the best interest of the employees, group, company, nation as well as your allies at heart, and that he or she is not a spy or a potential defector before divulging the pertinent secrets of the organization to them.

This is where you should also check the background, heart and motives of the potential successor. This is because there are usually many spy's that are so hard to be able to make out or uncover their true colors. You'll have to look up to the only One (God) who truly knows the hearts of every person and those who are wolves masquerading as sheep, to expose their true nature and identity.

Self -Aggrandizer or Promoter

Scrutinize to ensure that the incoming successor is not after self-aggrandizement - making it all about their personal promotion. I had a great leader and predecessor in the Pharaoh, so that I easily picked up the trait of not promoting my personal self or agenda over that of the people, group or nation I was being given charge of.

The fact that the Pharaoh was willing to step down from being referred to as 'God', and allow the One true God to be God over his people, was a very humbling experience and learning process for me. And, boy, was I even more dumbfounded that he would also declare me - a foreigner, slave and condemned 'convict', as the wisest in Egypt; because he perceived that the Spirit of the Most High God was fully and actively operating in and through my life.

Unwarranted and Unhealthy Competition

Unfortunately, too many people do not know where to limit their competitiveness. Competition is a good thing as it usually challenges and encourages innovation, ingenuity, growth, diligence, hard and smart working. Competition is however counterproductive and destructive when it replaces teamwork or synergy.

'Healthy competition' is often being encouraged in many places with 'winners' getting rewards while 'losers' get nothing; until they 'wake up' or wise up' to 'play the game' or 'play the system'; so as to move out of the 'losers club' into the 'successful club'. This has led to so much division, cut-throat tactics and out-right failures, as those who were meant to complement one another simply go on to compete against one another.

That is why it is written that 'a family, house, group, people, organization, company or nation that is divided against itself (in competition against itself), will fall or fail'. Truly healthy competition is helpful, but it is a very thin line to walk on - many quickly fall off of it into fighting dirty anyway they can, in order to win. As some people say that they do not like to lose and will do the unthinkable when it comes to winning.

My ten half-brothers were willing to kill me, or sell me of into slavery because they wanted to win and be ahead of me in life. I had dreams of the night that God had allowed me to have, about my eventually leading our extended family, even though I had ten older brothers. Those dreams of course didn't go down well with them. They couldn't pass up on the chance to finally become rich by selling me, their own blood brother, from the same ethnicity, race, nationality, family and humanity, off into the perpetual misery of slavery.

There are also many people who would quickly or eventually go into plotting and scheming the downfall of their immediate boss, leader, supervisor, manager, director, CEO, governor, president or king, when they find themselves in, or become promoted to a number two position like I experienced. God, through the Pharaoh, had promoted me into the number two position of the Prime Minister or Governor over Egypt, with only the Pharaoh being ceremonially higher than me. The second position however, just will never be good or excellent enough for some people.

His or Her Success, My Legacy

It's very key for outgoing leadership to understand that the success of the new and incoming leadership will solidify their own success and legacy. Who would want to put the continuity and success of the organization into the hands of someone who would soon likely run it aground? Most of the time, outgoing leaders do not die when they handover leadership to a successor; they usually may still live for a long time after. The families of the outgoing leader are likely to still be around with the outgoing leader, and both of them would likely still remain as a part of that organization, group or state, for a while.

This means such outgoing leaders still need the continuous success of the organization for the continuous livelihood or survival of their own generations to come. And if they do not need such livelihood support, they definitely would need to see the continuous success of what they used their whole lives to build or support.

If only many outgoing leaders take it to heart that the success of their successor is their most important accomplishment, that will also go a long way in determining their own future and that of their legacy, it would definitely help them to do everything possible in their power to ensure the continuity and success of their successor.

If a company, group, family, state or nation fails because you intentionally did not handle the succession process well, or you deliberately botched it, then your pensions or continued payments from the organization would also fail along with the company or group; and the memory of you leading the organization at some point in time, and all the 'great' work you did there perishes with the failure of the organization or state.

Chapter 7

Here Comes The Money!

Too Much Money?

When the Lord used the Pharaoh of Egypt to lift me up literarily out of the dungeons of life into the position of the second most powerful person in the world, for the very first time in almost two decades, huge amounts of money started coming regularly to me. I had legally become a billionaire in a day. Wow, I couldn't believe the amount of money coming to me as a billionaire.

Coming from nothing to so much money, I had to ask myself, 'is there something as too much money'? Well, you get to decide for yourself. Would you say a few trillions is too much for one person? Because that is where I am obviously headed as a person, I would say 'no, a couple of trillions is not too much'. Did I hear you say that it is because you're sure that I have no idea how much a couple of trillions of dollars or whatever your own money currency is, is the reason why I am saying it's not too much.

A Trillionaire in dollars would be able to give over $100 to every single person alive on earth and still have money left in his or her coffers. Assuming such a person lives up to 100 years old, then the person would have to live over 27 lifetimes of spending $1,000,000.00 a day to be able to use up his or her first trillion dollars. John D. Rockefeller was reported to have been worth more than half of a trillion dollars (about $664 billion) and was able to comfortably retire for the last 40 years of his life. He was arguably one of the richest men that ever lived.

King Solomon however was reported to have been the first and only Trillionaire that ever lived, which I beg to disagree on and you would be able to decide for yourself after you are done reading about what the Most High did for me. King Solomon was reported to have been worth over $2,000,000,000,000,000.00 (trillion); and his wealth made silver to become like a common stone you find on the ground that had no real monetary value.

The leading world authorities today have however rightly predicted that the person that would become the world's first (modern day) Trillionaire is already alive today; and that there would likely be more than 10 Trillionaire's in just a little over 50 from now. Their predictions however will likely fall terribly short because it did not take into cognizance the predictions of the Almighty God for the next 50+ years that there will actually be only one Trillionaire ruling the world in a one world government. We will get to that later on in this book or in a subsequent book later.

What You Do With Your Money Is Most Important

What you do with whatever money you make or that comes to you is the most important thing to making more money than how much money you have, don't have, or that someone else has. Many big conglomerates and businesses started with very little money that was put to efficient and maximized use to bring increase, growth and wealth.

Starting out with a great amount of money or with a great amount consistently coming in does not guaranty growth, increase or the building of wealth. Wastage or Mismanagement is the greatest enemy of growing wealth, or growing a company, family or a nation. Wastage is a very subtle devourer that many people have absolutely no idea about that it is in operation, until after a lot or everything has been lost. We will look into this a little later and deal fully with it in subsequent books.

As a person or a leader, would you say that you use your money to help others when they are in need or to oppress others that have less than you? Whether you believe it or not, your answer to that question will eventually either attract blessings and continuous increases to your money, or attract a curse and losses to your money. We will cover more on this later with my personal experiences.

I Became the first Trillionaire

When the Most High promoted me to become the official ruler over the most powerful nation of my time, Egypt, I became the second richest man alive - a billionaire. The beauty of that promotion that literarily blew my mind away was what happened over the next decade – the Lord gradually made me a Trillionaire in a much unexpected way.

The Lord had put dreams of leading my family into my heart, and that was the highest that any of us in my family of origin ever imagined that those dreams of the night represented. We had all interpreted the sun and the moon to represent my dad and mom also being under my leadership – one way or another, which we later found out to be a big understatement back then.

Your road to, or the process of your becoming wealthy, successful and fulfilling your dreams and goals may not be as rosy or comfortable as you would naturally want it to be. It may have some 'ups and downs', detours, land mines of cheaters, betrayers, and terrible definers or name callers. It may take much longer than you ever cared to have envisaged.

It may contain information that may be too difficult for you to decipher, understand or even want to accept as inevitable, or a part of the process of working it all out for our good. This is why the One Who knows tomorrows, and works all things out for our good, may not readily share all the details with us at different times.

Why He Only Shows Us a Glimpse

Sometimes the Lord will only give us just a glimpse into His purposes and plans for us and wouldn't give us further details for so many reasons. One of those reasons is the fact that we would tell those plans of His to the people closest to us, among whom will usually be spies, antagonist's, betrayers, murderer's and opportunist's like my half-brothers, and Judas Iscariot who sold Jesus off several decades later.

Just imagine the hatred and wickedness that was whipped up against me over just a glimpse of the future; I cannot begin to fathom what would have been brought up against me if people knew I was going to eventually rule the world sometime in the far off future. I'm sure my half-brothers would have chosen to out-rightly kill me as opposed to selling me into slavery, just like they originally agreed to.

At other times, He chooses not to tell us the process that leads to our dream actualization and fulfillment, because we would likely run away from it as far away as humanly possible, when we consider the challenges, heartaches, betrayals, loneliness, false accusations and every other bombshells or land mines that litter the way. Everyone seem to want the glory at the end, but not go through the story that leads to that glory.

Everyone wants a testimony, but not a test; a promotion, but no examination; receiving without giving; harvest without sowing or planting.

The Power of Patience

Patience is one of the fruit of the Spirit of God – evidence that the Spirit of God is present. It is one of the virtues and fruit that human beings naturally dislike and see no reason for. We wonder why God even refers to it as a virtue – a good character – and we really don't want God to teach it to us, put it in us, or grow it in us. We would rather have everything fast, faster and fastest.

Fast is what we naturally like, such that it is one of the most successful selling points in the world. Every year, newer models of cars, phones, computers, tablets, equipment's, appliances etc. are introduced and sold as 'faster', and man will quickly dish out an enormous amount of money to get the new thing that is faster by a nano-second than the one we had, which we barely used and just bought a few months prior.

The reality is that there are way too many important things that cannot be rushed in life and that we would need patience for. Decision making and relationships are two areas the successor, leader, and mankind in general, has to learn to handle with a lot of patience. Lack of patience leads to hasty decisions without considering all the necessary parameters involved. Too many bad decisions are made that have very devastating long term and widespread effects just because the decision maker 'did not have enough time' to go through all the needed information.

Mankind is at alarming rates of divorce – failures in marriages – just because people just 'don't have time for it anymore'. People are quick to want to get married but even quicker to want to get out of the marriage because building a successful marriage or relationship takes good time – years and years.

Many organizations want to either not have to 'spend the time' to train new employees properly, but to rather steal those that others took time to train and develop. Most incumbents or organizations want successors that they do not have to 'waste their time' to groom or cultivate into a success, because they want to move on quickly to other things.

Growth hormones are used to make agricultural produce – plants and animals used for mankind's foods – to grow really big in a very short period of time. Unfortunately, in our efforts to produce foods and raise animals faster and faster, we indirectly started producing cancer causing foods and livestock's that are leading to more deaths over time than any other cause of deaths. All because we want everything 'now', without the 'pains of' having to wait.

So many unwarranted quarrels, fights and wars are started at different times just because someone just is not patient enough to consider all the facts involved, but rather chose to 'move quickly', or to 'strike while the iron is hot'. How many people have later spent the rest of their lives in regret over hasty or too quick decisions, that didn't wait for all the facts of the matter to be made available?

There are so many married couples who rather choose not to have any children of their own, even when they are capable of having children, just because of the several years it will take to raise a child from infancy to adulthood, before their eventual independence from the parent. Many people would rather wish we could 'clone' full grown human beings and be done away with the 'painstaking day to day need', involved in raising a child, so that the adults can 'quickly' move on to other 'more important' things (fun).

Even many adults who choose to intentionally have children walk away from continuing to raise those children because 'it was taking way longer than they expected'. If we could, many mothers-to-be would readily opt for a one month 'full term' pregnancy that really wouldn't 'show' on their physique, as opposed to the long and arduous normal nine month length of a regular full term pregnancy.

Kind of hard to blame them because many hubbies (husbands) quickly seem distracted with their wives growing 'out of proportion' and 'losing shape' during and after pregnancies; and boy o boy, not to even talk about all those stretch marks that show up on their bodies after the delivery! Many men even start looking elsewhere at other women whose shapes have not been affected or 'marred' by pregnancy.

Funny thing is that such men love to have children born to them from their wives so much, but do not want to face the realities of the normal temporary and permanent changes that the pregnancy will have on their wives' bodies. And the wives are not left out as they seriously crave to have their own babies, but want nothing to do with the 'big belly' that throws their once alluring shapes into 'whack'.

Making Money may take some Time and Patience

Many people are too much in a hurry to 'succeed', make a lot of money, and keep the money from 'leaving' them. The reality of it all is that such kind of haste usually leads to people becoming willing to do terrible things and cut corners that shouldn't be cut, in order to achieve such wealth.

And people convince themselves that they will get away with any repercussions from the unconscionable and terrible things they do to others just to be rich, be the boss, get the edge, win the game or competition, or whatever it is they are willing to do wicked things for. Because each person usually believes we are smarter than everyone else.

Respectfully, but necessary to share is the painful example of the financial and investment leader who headed what is reported to perhaps be the largest Ponzi scheme or securities investment fraud (419) ever in U.S. history. He is serving a 150 year jail term while his two sons have both passed away before reaching age 50 - one from suicide and the other from lymphoma (cancer).

The man is 76 years old now, and makes $40 a month in prison, while a few years ago, the investment company he built controlled billions of dollars. Sadly now, he has no son's to carry on his name or legacy, or to be present at his burial when he dies. His estranged wife is said to now live in a one bedroom rented apartment that is less than 1,000 square feet and does not visit him in jail anymore after the suicide of their son. The painful question is: Was the looting and cheating worth this painful emotional end?

Some will look at my life and say that I had come into wealth overnight when I became the second world's most powerful person alive; and that I don't know what it was to work long and hard to try to be successful and wealthy without cutting corners and cheating to get ahead of the game. The reality is that I do know and do remember vividly my own painful years of toiling with nothing to show for it – remember that I was a slave or 'property' for several years with no pay or benefits.

I also do remember several 'opportunities' to cut corners and time, in order to get my great dreams and ambitions fulfilled, but had refused such with the help of the Most High, by trusting Him, and being patient while He worked it all out for me over the decades. I remember the countless 'opportunities' to be dishonest and cheat my task master, General Potiphar, after he had put me in charge of everything he owned, and he no longer kept record of them.

I remember his wife 'sweetly' telling me that I would become very rich quickly if I choose to have an affair or infidelity with her. I remember the allure of ruling over the stunningly rich and organized gang-controlled prison system that I was made the unofficial Warden of – I only needed to have played along with the system to have gotten super rich and powerful quickly. I chose to rather 'do to others what I would want others to do to me'. So, I did pass up on plenty of 'opportunities' at breaking God's laws and becoming my own 'God'. Will you do the same?

Chapter 8

The Best and Most Profitable Investment Product(s)

Crashing Stock Markets?

There is almost an uncountable number of investment products all over the world; yet, countless more are being developed on a daily basis. This brings to mind the following questions: What is wrong with all the countless investment products all over the world that is warranting the development of more countless ones? Why is there also a continuous **crashing** reoccurrence of the stock markets that all these investment products trade on, every now and again? And why do the crashes lead to many people losing their hard earned moneys and investments?

The monopoly power of the financial industry stems from the fact that every other industry or other parts of the economy are connected to and dependent on the financial industry in order to carry out their own transactions; and that leads to an undue edge of the financial industry on every other part of the economy.

Fraudulent practices in the financial industry indirectly leads to fraud in other industries as they are all connected to and indirectly dependent on the financial industry. This was why the housing industry collapsed in America's 2018 because those in the financial industry developed wickedly terrible Adjustable Rate Mortgages (ARM), and sold it to majority of those buying homes.

The ARM was designed to cheat millions of hardworking American's of their investment in a home and a roof over their heads. Those that wrote the loans were aware that their accomplices in government would continue to adjust the prime interest rate upwards regularly, and they would in turn be able to adjust the mortgage rate and payments upwards until the homeowners can no longer afford to make payments to keep a roof over their heads.

Then the banking and finance representatives would take back the homes in a foreclosure proceeding from the homeowners (everyone that borrowed money from the banks to buy their homes - the greater percentage of people), get paid from the insurance companies also for the 'lost revenue' on when they bank is working out the selling of the home to a new buyer; and so starting off the vicious circle again, and again.

The elected law makers (senate and representatives), law interpreters (judges and attorneys) and law executioners (government officials and law enforcers), however live large off of the 'generosity's' of the monetary or kind contributions that the financial industries 'graciously' gives to them in order to secure making laws that continue to support their 'enslaving' the rest of the populace (the 99%), and their avoiding being brought to justice for such wrongs against the people they are supposed to be leading.

How does the stock market crash without the intentional manipulation of some 'smart' people in the financial industry that collude with government officials? Do you see a skyscraper or a ramp just crash every now and again? No, because it has so many supporting pillars built to ensure it stays upright for decades and centuries with proper regular maintenance.

How are many financial institutions able to continue to get away with 'legally' cheating the general working populace time and time again? How are they able to stay in business even when caught and made to pay millions of dollars in fines? Because most of the overseeing bodies of authorities are regularly 'gifted' or paid to literarily look the other way; away from their fraudulent malpractices.

How is it that the banking and investment companies and their officials keep getting richer and paid more and more when everyone else in the society are losing their monies during such financial stock exchange crashes? Simply because these financial officials that connive or conspire with government officials set up the system to pay themselves even more during such times, and leave everyone else empty handed.

So many investment products are rigged and fraudulent with most of their fees 'legally' hidden and undisclosed. People are not told of the amount of fees that get taken out of their investments because the lawmakers have 'legally' enabled such cheating in exchange for 'political contributions' from those stealing from the general populace (those that they were elected by and whom they are supposed to be watching out for).

The stock market is supposed to naturally be guided by the very simple laws of demand and supply; the prices of an item go up when there is not enough supply of the item in question, but the prices go down once the supply is beefed up to meet or exceed the demand. But most company officials prefer the prices to keep going up unnecessarily by intentionally creating shortages for pent up demand. They prefer the supernormal profits that are really unsustainable because you can only milk the people as far as they can afford it and still remain sane.

The safest and most reliable investment product is also the simplest, and never complicated. It is what I also applied to become a Trillionaire. That product is thankfully available to everyone at their different financial levels in their life's journey. When I started using this product for the national good, I also made sure that the general populace also had the same opportunity of using it for their personal betterment. Though most people failed to use it, I still saw to it that they were taken care off during challenging times that later followed. That investment product is simply called *savings*.

Save-a-logy 101

Savings is such a simple tool that cuts across literarily every industry and facet of life. It works very well for the individual, family, company, groups, states or nations. Savings simply means putting aside some of the consumables (food, monies or any other thing) that come in for you today so as to use it on a later date when you may not have any consumable that comes in for you during that period.

Anyone and everyone can save and store up what they can depend on later on in life today. Savings does not require any particular level of education or sophistication. It simply is carried out by putting aside your money or food to be used or eaten at a later date when you really need it.

The basis of savings is to channel what would likely be wasted today, into tomorrow when it can meet needs that simply may not be met at that time. Many times, the food, monies or any consumable that comes to us today may be more than we can actually use up today; and so it will be wise to save the unneeded or excess portion today so that it will come in handy to be used tomorrow or at a later date when it is really needed, but it isn't coming-in at such later time.

Because saving is such a basic way of ensuring you have something to spend, eat or use later on in life when you don't have any of such food or monies coming in, it is made to look foolish and unattractive by many financial companies and those that work for them. As soon as a person's savings in the banks begins to grow, the banking and investment officials begin to hound them with the 'need' to 'grow their money faster' and 'at a higher rate of return' that usually are not feasible, sure or guaranteed.

Rather than encouraging people to save adequately over their productive lives to be able to have something to fall back on in their later years of retirement when most people are too old to work and to make a living, banks and brokerage officials promise to multiply the little people put in with them.

But when they have collected the monies of millions of people and they are not able to deliver the promised multiplied returns or amounts, they orchestrate a crash that losses peoples retirement monies while they still get paid hefty commissions and bonuses, especially during the losses. The question to ask is 'where or to whom do all the monies lost during stock market crashes, or recessions go to?'

Let's look at how we developed a lifestyle of savings from God's revelations and how it saved our whole nation and practically the world when the time of famine or lack of productivity eventually arrived. This is a principle that is laid down by God Himself for all of mankind and it works for any person, group of people or nation that uses it appropriately.

First, the Productive Years

Remember that the dreams God gave to the Pharaoh indicated that the seven (7) years of plenty or abundant productivity were going to come first before the later years of famine or non-productivity will show up. This has been laid down in the normal life cycle of mankind as we first become youths and young adults that have well developed brains and physical strength that must be put to productive use over the time of adulthood.

Then will come the later years of old age when we are no longer able to exert as much brain and physical strength to produce as we did when we were younger and in our prime years. What we do during those prime years or years of productivity will go a long way to determine what will happen to us and our loved ones during the later years.

I must tell you that there will always be some exceptions to every norm though; and God reserves the right to decide when to bring about those exceptions. These are exceptions where a person's training for their most productive years is prolonged extraordinarily through their youth and prime years to their much later years when most people have retired.

God does such when He wants to bring about exceptional productivity in such peoples old age, and He doesn't want anyone to think it was such peoples own natural productivity or achievement that is at play. He wants everyone to know that such great productivity only comes from Him and so His glory must not be attributed to such people that He uses to bring about such extraordinary results.

A little of that exception also applied to my life in the sense that when my age mates were going to regular 'schools' or learning centers and graduating to work and get paid to save towards their retirement, I was going through the school of slavery and incarceration because my productivity was going to affect many nations later on, and God didn't want anyone – myself inclusive – taking that credit to themselves.

For others, like Moses, whose destiny's productivity was to deliver the whole nation of Israel from slavery, that destiny was 'delayed' until he was eighty (80) years of age when he could no longer physically fight or exert aggressive energy. Moses had wanted to physically fight to bring Israel out of slavery approximately forty (40) years earlier in his prime. That initial attempt had led to him intentionally killing an Egyptian taskmaster or slave master, who was also intentionally oppressing 'his' slave.

Moses then fled into exile for the next forty (40) years, during which he gave up on that dream of delivering 'his' - actually God's - people from slavery. He was now old and not able to fight as he could have when he was forty years of age. But God wanted him and everyone else to know that it was not any man's physical strength, agility, prowess, strategies or fighting abilities that would lead to the deliverance of Israel.

David was also anointed to be king over Israel as a young man, but his reign did not take place until about twenty (20) years later when he had successfully completed his God appointed wilderness trainings where he also had to learn that it was not by his own powers or wisdom that he would be leading God's people or to become the greatest king in Israel's history; before the coming of the King of kings several generations and centuries later.

During your young adult and productive years, you will likely make a lot more than you can use by yourself or your small family. Do not waste what comes in for you, but save a good part of it, at least 20%, for the later years of retirement, famine or lack of productivity. And during the times of real abundance, save even much more than the 20% (40-60%), as much as possible.

The Pitfall of Pride

A major challenge to saving, however, is pride, which is a breeding ground for wastage and non-savings. There is a very unhealthy and foolish mentality that anyone who saves must be 'poor', for them to be worrying about savings. This is especially true about food and the developed nations of the world. The amount of food that the average family in developed nations waste per day is unbelievable and mind-boggling.

Most children in schools hardly eat one third of their school breakfast and/or lunches, and throw away the rest of it on a daily basis. Once a child sees another child wasting his or her lunch, and 'looking or feeling cool' while doing so, he or she quickly copies the same behavior 'just to look and feel cool' too. Many of them then go home and repeat their wastage performance on the food at home while 'looking and feeling pretty cool'.

Many children are being provided free breakfast and lunch in school by the government through the tax payer's moneys, and because the child or the parent is not directly paying for the meals, it doesn't pinch them or hurt them in any way when they waste the food. And because they have not gotten to school one day to be told that there was no breakfast or lunch because of the wastage over the past years, they never see any reasons to eating up their food, as opposed to wasting it.

The point here is *not* about not making food available to school children, but about stopping the billions of dollars in wastage of the food that school children throw away every day. Families and parents are not left out in this 'wastage' as opposed to 'saving' mentality. Even though most houses have refrigerators, freezers and constant electricity in developed nations that can be used to preserve leftovers from meals, most parents do not encourage or enforce saving such meals for either later in the day, or the next day. If they did, they would be able to warm up the preserved or saved meals to eat later.

There is a major lesson for us to learn from when Jesus fed five thousand people by multiplying a boy's lunch, in the fact that he asked them to gather the remaining food and preserve it for later consumption. This was also repeated when he fed four thousand people, that he asked them to keep the left over from wastage. Even if you choose not to believe in Jesus as God, still ask yourself why someone who could multiply just one person's meal to feed thousands of people whenever he needed to, still instructed the people to save the remnant of their food for later consumption?

It is because there will always be different seasons at different times in the lives of each individual, family, group, corporation, people or nation. There will be seed times (time to plant, work or be productive), and harvest times (times of eating and retirement). You cannot switch the seasons around to where you go through harvest before going through planting time; this is simply what those that like to cheat and defraud others want to do; especially many fraudsters in government, leadership and the financial investment, brokerage and banking world.

That is also what many slave 'owners' pride themselves in being 'smart' to do – have their slaves work while they get the harvest. They also go on to 'reassure' themselves that they 'paid' for the slave – of course they paid someone else and not the enslaved person. Another form of modern enslavement is where people from foreign countries are wooed with a better life they would get if they play in a 'free' lottery for the chance to migrate to that country and become citizens.

The unconscionable thing is that such people are then asked to advance a huge payment (several hundreds to thousands) ahead to the nation and must have people who would be financially responsible for their travels and assimilation into their potential new nationality. Isn't a lottery supposed to provide a huge payout to winners, whose initial investments were extremely minimal, as opposed to demanding a huge upfront payout from 'winners'?

Chapter 9

Wisdom is Most Important

Reading In-Between the Lines

The first seven years of abundant production of crops soon started in Egypt as God had revealed to and through Pharaoh, and interpreted to and through me. Remember, God is the Owner and Interpreter of His dreams or plans in the earth, but He will reveal and interpret them to and through whoever He chooses to. And as I had initially advised, we started saving at least 20% of the total production in all of the different cities. We built several storage facilities to save all the excess crops, grains and produce.

This is where wisdom is very much needed for each individual, family, corporation, group and nation. When some of the Egyptians observed us as nation -

the Egyptian nation, of which I was now a citizen of –
saving for the later years of famine and non-
productivity, they also took a cue and started saving
for their individual selves, families, corporations and
states. Sadly, very few did such personal and
individualized savings though.

Most people said that there could never be a time of
famine given the extraordinary level of productions of
harvest that the then current plantings were yielding.
They said it was beneath them to be 'struggling' to
save leftovers as only the 'poor' should care about
saving leftovers. 'As a matter of fact', they continued,
'the leftovers are actually meant for the poor'. 'Why
save food from yesterday, last week, last month, or last
year, when new and better looking food keep showing
up every new day at a rate far much faster than we can
consume or eat them'?

And there is a level of pride that also says 'I've got to
have the new thing, even when the hardly old one
works perfectly well'. New phone every year or even
every few months. New car models every year, new
wearables and gadgets, new clothes, shoes,
accessories, jewelry, and new of everything you can
possibly think of. 'Who needs the old, when you can
always have the new?' The 'old stuff' is really
supposed to be for the 'losers'.

The irony about new gadgets these days is that the supposed 'old' stuff are still working long after several newer iterations have died. Old appliances– microwaves, television sets, refrigerators, freezers etc. – are still working in many grandparents and great grandparents houses while the children's (younger) families have had to change their own newer appliances several times over already because they just do not seem to last more than a few years, while others barely last a few months.

The older grandparents cars are still going strong with just regular maintenance that do not go beyond oil change many times, while the newer children's cars equipped with so many gadgets and 'bells and whistles' have to keep going back into the dealership's shop every now and again, because of a 'glitch' or need for an 'update' to fix 'bugs', or to replace 'parts' that barely last for even a fraction of the time that the ones in the old vehicles lasts for.

Billion Dollar Advertisement Industry

And then billions of dollars are now required to advertise all these 'newer' items that we do not really need, and sell them to us as 'a must have'. If people do not have the new 'thing', they feel like failures and unsuccessful in life. People are being sold into becoming 'couch potatoes' of being able to sit in one place and control everything they have in the house with their voices and so called 'assistants'. It's like our fingers need to rest from touching the screen of a phone to make a call or search the web or click the TV remote buttons, when we can 'do it with our voice'.

An advertisement even touts many people saying 'I don't want to do it' back and forth between two grown-ups, until they 'wise up' and use their voice to ask a 'virtual assistant' to do it for them. Yet, the billion dollar exercise, weight-loss and health industries tell us to make sure we are exercising every day and stay active. But the tech industry seeks to take physical activities completely away from everyone – from the virtual assistants, to the virtual driving cars that should take away the 'stress and hassles' of us 'having to drive ourselves'.

Sabotage of the Manufacturing Industry

The manufacturing industry has undergone massive sabotage over the years as more and more products that are no longer durable are being made and 'shoved down the consumer's throats'. The manufacturing companies figured out that 'why would consumers or people buy newer versions of appliances, gadgets, phones and vehicles when their old appliances and cars are still functioning very well'?

And they decided such things shouldn't be made to last for too long so that the people would have reasons to buy the newer versions quicker and several times over in their lifetimes. Why sell a cell or mobile phone for $1,000.00 and have it last for 3-6 years before the person buys another one when you can have them purchase a new one every 1-2 years for $1,000.00 each (the average lifespan of many new phones, refrigerator, televisions, microwaves or dishwashers)?

Deceptions in the Credit System and the FICO Credit Score

The credit based system is made to look and sound so great and beyond everyone's wildest dreams for getting almost anything you want now and paying for it much later. And the advertising that encourages the use of credit is ever unrelenting and always in your face everywhere you turn.

'Buy now, pay nothing for three months'; 'Buy now, pay no interest for 3 years'; 'Buy now, pay over 6 years'; 'Buy now and its $0 down payment, $0 first month payment, $0 delivery fee; $0 installation fee, $0 haul away fee, $0 application fee, $0 installment fee, $0 origination fee, $0 any other fee you can think of, just so long as you come as get this 'thing' – phone, appliance, TV, furniture, car, time share, computer, tablet, vacation, vacation home, condo, house, pent house, wearable, smart watch, or whatever it is that catches your fancy or makes you feel 'you have arrived'.

Banks and financial institutions also peddle credit with so many entrapping adverts like: 'You've earned it, now take the card and do whatever you want with it – take a vacation, buy whatever you want with it at any time; 'It's your money, do whatever you want with it'; 0% APR for 18 months, 0% annual fee, 0% balance transfer fee; You're specially invited to apply for this card'; 'No Credit Limit, just buy anything at any time, whatever the price'; Get cash from it and spend it as you like'; Same as cash'; 'Only for the select few that qualify'.

The catch is that you really didn't earn the buying power or credit the banks and financial institutions are extending to you, because you didn't work for it and it is never the same thing as cash. You will have to pay the financial institutions back for the amount of *'your'* money – actually *'their' money* – which you spend when the bill becomes due at the end of each month.

The biggest catch, however, is that once the 0% interest rate is over, your minimum required monthly payments back to the financial institutions skyrocket to the point that most people find it difficult to continue paying it. The required amount to pay back jumps up to about 3 times the amount you used to pay because the interest rates jumps to anywhere between 15% and 29%. And once you can't make the minimum monthly payments, the financial institutions do a 180 degree turn from being all so sweet and 'serving', to the debt collector and mean mode.

The banks and financial institutions then accelerate the repayment timeline for what you owe them. This means that they demand a bigger part of the loan, or even all of the loan, to be immediately repaid to them. They all of a sudden seem to just discover from your missed payments that you are no longer their darling or don't want to ever pay them again; even though you had been their on-time paying customer for several months or years.

The strange thing is that your missed payments were not surprises to the financial institutions because they already knew you would likely not be able to keep up that payment over extended periods of time (like 7 years for a car or 30 years for a home). So they already took out insurance against 'if' – actually, when – you get to that inglorious milestone. They will get paid for your 'failure' that they knew was only a matter of time – due to the predatory nature of the loan.

They then sell off your debt to debt collectors who will use every lie and threat in the books of lies to make life miserable for you until you look for the money to pay them; while the financial institutions spend more money and time advertising to 'haul-in' the next 'scape goat'. Yet, the financial industry will still write off the debt at the end of the financial year as a loss, so that they also evade paying taxes on the amount - of course legally because the politician friends they regularly contribute to make the laws that allow them to do those things 'legally'.

Then the collection agencies start calling on time-barred debts - debts already past the number of years the law allows collectors to call on. They will also call relations, neighbors and everyone possible in order to 'locate', or better still, harass people who never had any direct contract, transaction, or agreement with them initially or at any given time. They will also call at odd hours of the day outside of time allowed by the law.

And the most sad aspect of all these negative practices of the financial industry and their supporting industries – law makers, law interpreters, law enforcers, advertising groups and collectors – is the fact that their biggest targets to defraud are the internationals who were told that they had won a visa lottery and would be able to now access 'the 'National' Dream' as an immigrant.

The reason the immigrants are the major targets of many industries, especially those they seem inevitable to avoid – financial, medical, housing and schooling – is because they usually migrate with the notion that they are coming to a nation that welcomes them as 'lottery winners' and that they would find the greatest hospitality and help once they arrive.

You'll be shocked to know that immigrants are not offered even an ordinary bottle of water, not to mention anything else (snack or meal) during the several waiting hours in which they cannot go out to get a drink or something to eat before the beginning of the ceremony to swear them into becoming citizens – now that is just plain cold and typical of how you treat someone whom you claim is welcome, but your basest of actions shows otherwise.

Immigrants are the ones who are usually not conversant of a credit based societies intricacies on the use and management of credit; and so they easily fall prey to the whims and caprices of several sales professionals who shove everything they do not need down their throats with the promise that they really need those things.

And let's not even get started on the credit score referred to as the FICO score. The FICO score and credit report is supposed to tell how well a person can take on debt or credit to pay for what he or she has not worked for, and to pay it back over time 'responsibly'. Yet the barrage of adverts and compulsion to use credit is unrelenting. The banks and financial institutions however are not penalized or fined for not issuing credit 'responsibly'; they actually get rewarded for it by getting tax breaks and right offs at the end of the year.

The individual who however did not use credit 'wisely', gets negative connotations put on their credit files and reports by the lending banks and financial institutions. Such negative connotations now make it even more difficult and very much more expensive for such individuals to get a job or finance basic necessities of life like a house or a vehicle to move them from one place to another in this global village; and especially for work to be able to earn a living.

The FICO score and credit report have shown over decades that they are the biggest tools of enslaving people unnecessarily in debt. The higher your credit score, the more people are cajoled into taking on way bigger debts that they are more and more likely to default on; because such larger debt are way over their income levels and ability to pay.

A man said his credit score is over 800 and he confessed that his debt are way over his head to repay (over $1 million). He had been bombarded with false advertising of 'it's your money, do what you like with it'; but now that the creditors are calling day and night, he has realized a little bit too late that he had been fooled into erroneously building a lie for himself – a great credit FICO score, as opposed to building real wealth and a good net worth.

Many great nations have also bought so much into this lie of the credit system, and have borrowed billions of dollars over decades, but spent such national debts on frivolities and unnecessary things of life. Many borrow for festivities, events and competitions that will end-up not bringing profits or returns to them that are commensurate to or higher than the amounts of money they had borrowed to build facilities and get security for such events.

So many nations have also contributed one way or another to the destabilization of many other nations with covert operations where they have 'played god' in interfering in the political processes, elections and sovereignty of these other nations. Their purpose is to set up into government, people who have absolutely no clues about running a country or putting its natural resources and manpower to the best use; so as to be able to plunder such peoples resources and manpower under the guise of 'aids' – helping them.

Chapter 10

Successfully Handling Lack of Productivity

Then Came the Years of Famine or Lack of Productivity

A time of famine or lack of productivity - no marriage proposals, no marriage, broken courtships, no child, no academic success, no business or job success, no promotions, no real friendships, no helpers, no money, no medical cure, no agricultural harvests, no technological successes etc. - can be very challenging for anyone (and everyone experiences one or another at some point in their lifetime) that experience the differences faces of it.

And a very challenging aspect is the fact that even for different people who experience the same kind of lack of productivity (or challenge, failure, set-back, loss, famine, poverty, scandal, set-up or 'set-down' etc.), it usually will have some slight differences, individuality or uniqueness to it that makes it uncommon; even though there may be many aspects of it that are general and common to everyone that experiences it. But none of it is a surprise to God and to those that will listen to Him.

And as God had revealed, the 7 years of great productivity, wealth, abundance, surplus and harvest soon came to an end, and was followed by the 7 years of lack of productivity, famine, poverty, agricultural and manufacturing failures. It was like nothing ever seen or experienced in the great nation of Egypt since its inception.

Crops barely had to touch the ground during the years of great productivity in Egypt, before they would sprout up and grow healthily into great harvests without much effort of anyone really tending to it. Such success had of course quickly attracted pride into the hearts of the people and they had celebrated *'their'* success, ingenuity, hard work, prowess, wealth, academic and technological advancement'.

I would later find out that these two great phenomena of the years of plenty (great national success) and the years of lack (failed agriculture), were not just unique to Egypt, but were experienced all across the world or globe. And I also discovered that they were natural cycles that were prevalent in the history of the world.

God had said long ago that while this current earth exists (and He's promised to build a new one later when the current one is destroyed by man's own handiwork), there will always be different opposing seasons of seed time and harvest time; with the choices you make in each one having a profound effect on the other.

God had promised He would not smite or destroy the whole earth and its people anymore after the flood He sent in the time of Noah wiped out everything except Noah, his family and the animals he had preserved based on the instructions of God. Even though God has also revealed that mankind will eventually experience tremendous judgement to the earth and the heavens (1st and 2nd heavens – the earth's sky and outer space beyond the earth where the sun, moon, stars and other things like asteroids are), later due to man's pride and rejection of God.

The wonderful thing is that man rejected putting their lives in the Hands of God, but mankind is cool with making artificial intelligence to help carry out the great things that we are not able to carry out ourselves. But man has also chosen to disregard the existence of evil forces (Satan and demons), or acknowledge their existence but disregard that they are beyond man's control, and are able to take over man's natural and 'artificial intelligence' just like they currently take control of so many human beings who allow them and help them to carry out unimaginable feats of wickedness and evil toward animals and other people.

Man has built enough fire power against other nations and people that is able to bring the world down to its very knees. Mankind has also been racing to achieve and perfect artificial intelligence (AI - self-governing intelligence that is still supposed to be subject to man). The artificial intelligence (AI), though meant to carry out good and great things for mankind, however will likely get hijacked by a glitch, a haywire self-written code, or just forces unknown as predicted in movies like 'The Terminator' movies, 'The Matrix' movies, and 'The Avengers: Age of Ultron' movie.

That 'glitch' or 'unknown forces' however, have been predicted in the Bible to turn out to be the forces of Satan and his demons; who by the way hate all of mankind with a great passion because we replaced them in the scheme of God. These forces will likely take over mankind's created stockpile of fire power and uses it against mankind and the earth later; all still carrying out God's judgement on wickedness.

The Worst Side of Mankind Comes Forward During Times of Lack of Productivity

Let's get back to the story of my life though. When the years of famine and barrenness came, nothing germinated in spite of our (man's) best efforts and technological advancement. The whole nation struggled and made sure that we were planting, watering, cultivating and doing everything possible to ensure the growth of the crops, but nothing worked.

This is where man's pride eventually becomes painfully obvious. When all of man's efforts fail, we then realize that we need help beyond our own selves and abilities. Unfortunately, even at such points, mankind will still look for help that they believe they can control - guns, bombs, WMD's, mystic forces, mediums, sorcery, dark matter, witchcraft, and/or artificial intelligence.

But Satan is far older than mankind and far 'wiser' or cunning and crafty, such that he makes mankind to believe that they can rebel against God and use his (Satan's) own mystic abilities, but yet remain in control. Satan is the perfect slave master, who makes a man a slave under himself while making such a person to believe that they are in control of their own selves, and that they are 'doing anything they want to do'; with no one higher than them deciding for them, or to answer to.

The famine and lack of productivity soon led to many individuals, families, groups, peoples and even nations to run out of what to eat or live on; and people started starving. After a while, people soon ran out of the little food that some had cared to save while the majority of others who were too proud to save anything at all, were the first set of people to start starving.

People who believed that saving food was only for the 'poor', now started trying to save the very little they could buy or lay their hands on. The problem however, was that the 'supermarkets and grocery stores' soon ran out of food to sell because their suppliers were running out of fresh produce to supply them.

The agricultural sector was quickly going bankrupt as they didn't have any more growth of any of their plantings and cultivation's. Then began the problem of serious hoarding - where even the farmers were refusing to release the little food they had left to the stores for sale. This was far off from artificial hoarding that many businesses do with their products - by creating an artificial scarcity in order to drive the price up obnoxiously to create supernormal profit for their executives - though they say it's for the shareholders.

This was real scarcity because nothing was simply growing in spite of everyone's best efforts to find a solution. A tea bag may look all nice and clean with a clear color when it is dry, but get it wet in hot water and you will see its hidden colors and capabilities come out. This simply is an analogy to depict the fact that people may show nice parts of themselves when things are dry and rosy or going good, but will show unbelievably terrible sides to them when things get hot, challenging or unproductive.

At such times of lack of productivity, many will resort to cheating, stealing, lying, killing and doing just about anything to survive or bring about some productivity or harvest. Many will take unbelievable extreme advantages over their fellow human beings. People will hoard food or charge outrageous amounts for the little food or water available. Some will even kill their own spouse or children and feed on them in order to survive. Some will go into the business of enslaving others and forcing them into labor to bring about new productivity.

Who will God Use to Help Me?

The people of Egypt soon approached the Pharaoh - the king and ruler of Egypt - for a solution to the scarcity of food all over Egypt. As the average citizen of Egypt prided themselves as being the greatest race or ethnicity that ever lived, with all other people far below their status, dignity, education and technological advancement; they made sure that they ignored the Pharaoh's decree and law that I was now the official and active leader of Egypt.

The Egyptians bypassed coming to me for a solution to the food scarcity because I was a 'foreigner' who they could easily distinguish from themselves. My obvious differences being - nation of origin, ethnicity, race, skin and eye color, hair and natural build, as well as accent.

They figured that they could get the Pharaoh to rescind his decision - as is typical of many people - made years earlier that I was now the person to direct the nation as its Governor. That position never existed before he created it for me under the directions of the

Most High God. They wanted him to break his word and lure him into taking back the 'power' or control of the nation from me.

But the Pharaoh made his word his bond – very uncommon in any day, age, race, or ethnicity. Most people will do anything to retain positions of power, authority, control, wealth, or success, and it doesn't matter to them whom they betray, sell out, cheat, maim, kill or destroy. Not this Pharaoh though as he directed them all back to me for the solution to the food scarcity.

The people complained bitterly and said they don't even want to have anything to do with that 'foreigner' you call our leader. 'He came to this nation as a slave and should only have remained a slave'; they retorted. 'Even worse off is the that fact that he is a convicted felon, who had attempted to rape one of the finest and most noble women of Egypt, and he should have been left to languish in jail or the dungeons till his sorry life ebbed out of him'; they continued.

The Pharaoh pointed out that there is a God who sees beyond all the lies and treacheries of every human being; and eventually exposes situations like mine where so many innocent people are usually framed for wrongdoing by others, so that the framed will take the fall for their wicked deeds. He explained that he had seen enough of perverted justice systems also where most judges are 'paid for' by the wicked in order to convict the innocent and acquit the guilty – more common than you would want to think or admit.

The Pharaoh simply advised them that he was not asking them to do what he himself had not done – submit to the leadership of the Most High God – Who had chosen to use the foreigner (me) to save their nation from what would have been a painful and slow destruction through famine. The Pharaoh told them it was a hard and futile thing for them to continue to refuse the care and leadership that the Almighty God was extending to them all through the foreigner called Zaphenath Paneah or Joseph.

'Besides', the Pharaoh had continued, 'this foreigner of a man called Joseph has been far more faithful and trustworthy than most people I've ever encountered everywhere – including our citizens and foreigners. He has had opportunities to steal our natural resources like most people do, but he has refused to go down that road'. 'Joseph has also had the opportunities of having affairs – sexual infidelity – both before and after marriage, but had chosen to submit to the laws of the Most High and turned his back on all such 'opportunities'; how many of you can say you've been faithful in even one of those two areas; not to mention in both areas?'.

All the delegates and leaders were initially silent and could not respond to the question of faithfulness in their leadership or marital positions. But just like it is typical of human beings being 'smart' or 'wise' in our own eyes or perspectives, they eventually said it was impossible for anyone to be faithful in not 'appropriating' some of the resources put in their care to their personal use, or to stay matrimonially faithful in an environment where they were being bombarded with nudity and mostly exposed bodies, which were indirect invitations to 'see and come-n-get it'; 'or why else do you think those bodies are being exposed?'; they retorted.

The Pharaoh then asked the leaders and delegates if they never wondered why he, the once upon a time 'God' of Egypt, stepped down from the aggrandized position of a man being referred to as 'God', on his own accord or volition, without a coup or fight against God when He revealed Himself to him in dreams of the night; and with the interpretation He gave through Joseph - a foreigner, slave and convicted felon? They replied that he sure seems to be 'reading' their minds in knowing their biggest unanswered question.

'Well, let me answer your biggest, yet never asked question', the Pharaoh said. 'I believe it is wisdom to willingly submit to the God of 'Gods' when you are confronted with gravely difficult challenges that no human being, groups of human beings, or groups of 'Gods' are able to solve or help you with; until someone shows up with the answer or solution, but he is humble enough to point to the fact that it is the Most High God that gave the answer or solution to the challenge', Pharaoh continued.

'You simply don't have the sovereign decision making power or autonomy of the Almighty God, because every other being came from Him and are subject to Him. Yes, it is true that He has given every creature He made the freewill to choose what they want to do; but He has also put laws in place to serve as guidelines to our decision making processes'.

'There are present, continuous, and forever positive or negative consequences to the choices we make. I have simply chosen to be on the side of the Almighty God and submit to His leadership, no matter who He chooses to use to Help me; I suggest that you do the same and go to Joseph, whom God has chosen to use to help us through this major death dealing famine'; the Pharaoh concluded.

Relating with People Who Don't Like You

I have discovered that there will always be people who do not like you and may never choose to like you, no matter what good things you do for them. There however will be some who may not like you today, but who will have a positive rethink over time or after some life-changing event(s), and then chose to become your friend, ally or helper.

We however need to rely on the leading, direction and revelations of the Spirit of the Almighty God about people, as we have seen in my case the situation where even members of a person's nationality, race, ethnicity, group, corporation, or extended or immediate family may choose to become an enemy.

When people allow wicked forces of Satan and demons to work through them, and become an enemy to you, you also have to look up to God for help and directions on how to relate with such people. For some, God may allow the enemies to 'get rid of you' for some time, so as to keep you away from their continuous attempts at your life - like my brothers sold me off into lands unknown to them.

For others, God may ask you to move away from them like He asked the earthly family of the messiah to move away from King Herod until he was taken out of the way. For others, He may incapacitate them so that they cannot hurt you, and then ask you to feed, clothe or be kind to them so that they may have a positive rethink about doing wicked things to others - like He did with the army sent to arrest Elisha.

And yet to others, God Himself will multiply His judgements and punishments on them until they are almost wiped away or completely wiped away, as seen later against a different Pharaoh who believed the Pharaoh of my time was 'chicken' to have stepped down from the 'God' position that he and his people had ascribed to him. That subsequent Pharaoh and the people of his day in Egypt then went on to discriminate against the Israelite-Egyptians, and to enslave them for over 400 years. They were almost wiped completely away by God when the harvest of their actions was fully grown.

It is however paramount that we do not go against God's decisions on how to relate with any person or group of people who chooses to make themselves enemies to us, so that we do not get in God's way when He starts dealing with them. This is so important because the natural thing is to want to revenge against those that hurt us, or to avenge ourselves; but that would however put us also in the line of God's judgement that is aimed at such enemies.

We cannot choose for anyone else what they will do and who they decide to become an enemy to; and we also cannot decide how and when God chooses to respond to such choices that people make. One thing we can however be sure of is that whatever each person does, say or chooses not to do or say, is a seed that is planted, and that will germinate over time to bring a harvest of the same kind later on to them; only in a larger or more pronounced return though.

It is very easy to however become sentimental and feel overly sympathetic for anyone or group whose negative harvest catches up with them. That is when we want to decry God for the negative harvest, and turn a blind eye to the evils and wickedness that the person or group had done or planted against others in the past.

I believe most of the Egyptian leaders did not want to also come back to me for help because of how they had treated me over the years as a slave, as a wrongfully convicted person, and as a person they had thrown away into the dungeons to rot away forever; their consciences weighed heavily on them and they were ashamed of their past actions.

They however had no other option but to come to me for their help because the Pharaoh refused to renege on the decision of making me the official ruler over the land. The next few years of the continued famine and lack of productivity became a steep learning curve for us all in Egypt and all across the world. God was teaching us all major lessons on the laws of sowing and reaping.

I opened the storehouses that held the preserved various grains and started selling food to the people all across the land of Egypt. But people from neighboring countries soon started showing up in our land and requesting for us to sell them some food. It soon became apparent that the famine was not limited to our nation alone, but was happening in the neighboring nations as well.

But as the years of famine progressed, other nations even farther away from our borders began to make long trips to buy food from us, and it soon became obvious that the famine had become a global phenomenon. People from every nationality, ethnicity, groups, corporations and even families were making several days' journeys to our land in order to buy food.

Truly, God is the God of all peoples and we are all His handiwork. He took me, an Israelite from a far-away land, to come and become a part of a supposed pagan nation of Egypt, in the most unusual way - conspiracy, slavery and a botched judicial system - and become it's leader under a supposed pagan Pharaoh who turned out to be more believing, humble and obedient to the voice of God than the people of my origin who were supposed to have been the people of God. And He did all that to save the world from perishing from a global famine.

Chapter 11

Wonders Will Never End

The Wonder of the Mighty Falling

As the Governor, Prime Minister or official Ruler of the land of Egypt, I made sure I personally oversaw the sale and distribution of the preserved grains. This was so that I could ensure that there were no wastages and 'leakages' or stealing, which is very common among us human beings. And am I so glad that I did not delegate this role as that would have likely made me miss the next wonder that God was about to show me.

There are a few reasons why the mighty may fall. One reason could be that such a person allows 'their' success to get them puffed up or become proud. When a person or a people become proud, they usually start to 'diss' or disdain being 'under' God or having to answer to Him. They then do everything possible to declare their independence from God.

God will however usually give them some time to rethink their actions as He reaches out in order to reason with them and bring them back under His loving cover. And so because there are no immediate repercussions that become apparent and evident to their error, they usually get more pumped up at the 'toothless bulldog' who calls Himself God, but seems to not be able to do anything about the evils they are carrying out.

After the ample reach out and time that the Almighty God gives in order to bring such people back under his love, He then goes on to humble them by allowing their so-called 'success' to fail them. This is yet a loving reach out to see if they will come back to their senses, and seek to return to the loving arms and cover of the Most High God. Some will take this reach out and come back under the cover of the Most High, while some will only increase in pride and declare that they would rather die than put themselves back under the cover and leadership of the Most High God.

As the number of international people needing to buy grain from us steadily increased, Egypt soon became the World Trade Center. People from every nation of the world were showing up on our national doorsteps and we had to set up what we called the Department of Homeland Security - an agency to ensure that the people coming to our national borders and requesting for help were really in need of help, and not spies in disguise.

Then one day, and completely out of the blues, the strangest of visitors showed up requesting to buy food. Why don't you go ahead and take a few guesses as to who it was that showed up? Well, nice try and great job if you guessed right - they were none other than my very own ten much older half-brothers.

Did I hear you ask if they were the same ones that sold me off into slavery over 2 decades ago? Yes, and those were the only half-brothers I ever had except if my dad got another wife and children with her after I was sold off; which is never far-fetched in my 'weird' family of origin - remember that my dad was married to my mom and her older sister, as well as their two maids, all at the same time.

I wish I could say that these were the last people on earth I could ever expect to see, except that I never even expected to ever see them again in my life-time, because of the circumstances that surrounding our parting ways. And I am very sure they never expected that they would ever see me again in their life-times either. Nobody ever expects to see a person that they sold off into slavery ever again - such a person is expected to die off pretty soon as most slaves die off due to the inhumane way their 'owners' use and treat them (work them to death, use them in blood sports like gladiator duels, or just lynch them off for the slightest reason or fun of it).

Remember that I even named our first son with the name 'Manasseh', with the meaning of 'God has made me forget all my past troubles and all of my father's household'? When the Lord God smiled down on me after He had put me through all the trainings of the schools of slavery and dungeons, and lifted me up to become the second in command to the Pharaoh, I never expected to ever set my eyes on any member of my family of origin anymore.

How awesome God truly is. These half-brothers of mine who had become rich decades ago by dealing me off into slavery, were now experiencing that their riches were of no value to them in their present day, since there was no food to buy in their country or other neighboring countries to theirs. The money that they had trusted in, became proud of from when they turned their backs on the Most High God, had eventually failed them.

And here they were on their knees in greetings to the official ruler of the nation of Egypt (their baby brother

- whom by the way they could not recognize, as I was now dressed as a true Egyptian ruler in great splendor). Suddenly, I realized the miracle of what had just happened - the indestructible dream that God had given to me in the visions of the night and in my goal making times a few decades back, had just become a reality - better still, God had made it a reality.

The dream that all the grains of my much older half-brothers would one day bow down before mine had just literarily happened before our eyes. This was a dream my half-brothers had vehemently kicked against because they had erroneously interpreted the dream to mean that they all were going to become my subjects or servants later on, as opposed to the true interpretation God was now bringing to pass - that their own grains and food supplies will fall to the ground or fail in the future, while mine will remain standing, or as if no famine was ever around it.

They had all formed the unholy alliance of hating my guts, dreams and ambitions to be great, as if those were my own ill-conceived aspirations, and as if I was really interested in their literarily bowing down to me. My ambition to be great was born out of my desire of helping people, as opposed to enslaving them. They believed that everyone - including me - had the same outlook of dominating or enslaving other people, just like they love to do; which was why their interpretations of my dreams then were laced with their deep-seated biases.

Never Give Up on the Dreams that God gave you!

I had literarily given up on that first dream ever becoming a reality because of my circumstances over the last two decades; but God had not forgotten or given up on the dream. He was actually working it out for my good and the general good of the world, as it was becoming apparent to me. He truly is a good and faithful God.

What would our nations (now I am a full citizen of Egypt and also of Canaan where I was born) have done to survive this drought, famine, natural disaster and widespread worldwide lack of productivity, if the Lord had not worked out my being here and working with the Pharaoh? God had guided us into saving tons and tons of food for such a time as this; a time that the good Lord had revealed was coming?

He had also been the only One Who had kept reassuring me in the deep crevices of my heart that He was still going to fulfill that dream, even when everything else pointed to the opposite. He knows the future because He is the Future - He is the same God yesterday, today, tomorrow and forever. He gives us the free will to either follow His lead or to do whatever seems good to us, but He will never abandon His position as the Most High God.

But then, what about my second dream that the interpretation my half-brothers and father gave to was the 'last straw that broke the camel's back'. That dream of the night that showed the sun, the moon and the eleven stars bowing down to me? They had interpreted that dream to mean that my father, mother and eleven brothers would be bowing down to me; and I thought to myself, 'that sure doesn't seem to be happening now; because my dad, mom and youngest brother are not here and I don't even know if they are still alive or not'.

So I decided to question my half-brothers further to find out about the rest of the family and also compare what they had to say about their backgrounds and what I know about them, even though they didn't still know that it was me. I alleged that they were spies that came to discover the weaknesses of our nation at a time like this when the whole world was coming to buy food from us.

Their replies were very informative. They said they were all children of the same father, twelve of them, but that the reason I also see ten of them is because one of them was 'no more' or dead (referring to me, unknown to them), while the youngest was back home with their dad who wouldn't let the young boy out of his sight - because the boys only other full brother had 'mysteriously' been killed by a wild animal and his body was never found, around the same age his younger brother is now.

I told them that I didn't believe a word of what they were saying and that I needed proof that they were saying the truth. I asked them all to stay behind in a detention cell, while one of them would be free to return to their homeland and bring that youngest brother for me to see and verify that he truly was their brother, and that they were not spies. 'So, who is it going to be to go and bring your youngest half-brother while the rest of you 'suspects' remain in custody?'

Over the next three days, they all dillydallied or wasted time over deciding who gets to go home free, as the freedom of the rest of them did not seem to be guaranteed, since their dad had promised himself that he would never allow the boy out of his sight, not to talk of travel to a faraway foreign country that none of them had ever been to before. And even if they were ever to bring their youngest half-brother, this

Egyptian ruler seemed mean and unlikely to be convinced.

After three days, I figured I had to make that decision for them, but decided to make it a lot easier on them too. I reversed my decision for only one of them to go home free to bring their youngest half-brother, to only one of them remaining behind in custody, while the rest were free to return home with food for their starving families and to bring the boy later. I told them that I was doing this because I feared God, and they all looked at me in pure astonishment on my talking about God because they regarded me as an infidel.

Every person's Actions will return to Bless or Haunt them later!

So I chose Simeon to stay behind in detention while the rest were freed to go back home. My choice seemed to boggle their minds in ways they just could not seem to wrap their heads around. They quickly started talking among themselves in their native language or vernacular – which, of course, they never expected anyone that was 'not' from their country of origin to be able to understand - especially an Egyptian ruler.

They asked among themselves how I seemed to have 'randomly' chosen Simeon. Simeon was one of the two very outspoken ones among them back then, and of the two referred to as 'hotheads' (always angry and bloodthirsty). Read more about him and his other brother (Levi) orchestrating the wiping out in cold blooded mass murder of almost all the males of an entire city because the son of the leader there had first raped their sister (Dinah) before asking for her hand in marriage, in the prior book titled *'Who Am I? Going Rogue: Discover and Become the Best You!'*

As a matter of fact, Simeon was the one who had broached the subject matter of getting rid of me by killing me over twenty years ago – read more on that in the second book, *"Who Am I? Big Dreams: Never Say Never About Your Dreams and Ambitions"*. He was the one who ventured the suggestion that the only way they can come out into 'their own success, fame or destiny' from being left far behind in my shadows as the miracle child of our family back then, was for them to plain and simply get rid of me for good.

He said I was the one that always 'stole' the limelight of every conversation back then in our family of origin; whether the conversation was just within the family, or even with others from outside. He had vented so angrily when they captured me back them that 'let's see what becomes of you and all this your so called dreams of greatness when we kill you now, show-stopper, because our own shows are just about to get started finally, after you're long dead and gone'.

Had it not been for the mercies of God through Rob (Reuben), our oldest brother, who wisely suggested that they should not spill my blood, but can actually derive much more pleasure in watching me starve to death in a pit over time; they would have gone ahead to out rightly kill me then.

I had thought that Reuben was so mean and wicked to have suggested a much slower and painful death for me back then, but as I listened to their conversation now in their vernacular, I could decipher that he had said that to the others in a bid to rescue me later behind their backs - which didn't happen because they sold me off into slavery while Reuben was away for a short time.

Reuben was telling them that He believes this unfortunate incidence that they were now going through - detention and having to decide who stays and who gets to go home free - were the harvests of all their actions over twenty years ago when they carried out wicked deeds against Joseph by attempting to out rightly kill him at first, and then going on to sell him off into slavery behind his back later.

The others quickly lashed out at Reuben pointing out that he shouldn't attempt to absolve himself of any blame because he should have provided the rest of them a more godly leadership as the oldest brother, and if only he had not been too timid to speak up and insist that they should not harm Joseph back then, maybe they would not be in their present precarious circumstance.

'Besides', they continued, 'you were the one that started the jealousy and hatred toward the boy when dad was always all-about Joseph, the tenth youngest son, and never about you the oldest among the children.

They all were however passing the blame around among themselves for what they had done against me years prior. Simeon shot back in anger that it was not his fault because he agreed not to kill me out rightly anymore when Reuben suggested the slow death through starvation in a dry pit; and so he believes the blame lies on Reuben. 'Besides, the ultimate blames should actually rest at the feet of the 'Whiz-Kid' Judd (Judah), whose suggestion to sell Joseph off into slavery, was the final option they had all opted for.

Then Judah shot back at them all that this was very typical of the rest of the brothers - finding someone else to blame for their misdeeds when things later turn negative and upside down. 'Weren't you all super excited when I made each of you rich from selling the boy back then? Didn't each of you collect your respective shares of the proceeds of the slave trade? Didn't you all spend the monies as you deemed fit individually? Aren't you all still spending from that money or the monies you made from investing that windfall?'

Owning up to Misdeeds and Seeking Forgiveness

They all kept quiet for a short time and could not respond to Judah's thought provoking questions as each person was faced with the undeniable facts that they all had been complicit in the wrong doings, and were guilty as charged by Judah. What however soon took me by surprise in their conversations among themselves was when they all spoke after the silence that had fallen over their arguments after Judah spoke.

They all soon seemed to agree that each of them had contributed in one way or another to their misdeeds against their younger half-brother, Joseph, back in the days. And they each reproved their own selves for their part in the collective unholy-alliance they had formed back then, and the atrocities they had committed.

Most shocking part of their conversation to me however was that they then went on to acknowledge the Most High God in their predicament - saying that they knew they were being punished by God (which of course is half the truth because they were actually reaping what they had planted themselves in prior years.

They went on to remorsefully recount among themselves their error in not listening to the harrowing and tearful pleas and appeals of their quite young half-brother - me, of course - year's back then when they were putting him through slave trade. My brothers that I remember back in the days, did not believe in the Almighty God as their actions back then showed; even though my dad had introduced us to God as we were all growing up.

They had all always pretended that they believed and followed God back then just for the fun of feeling 'smart' in being able to deceive dad that his children were believers in the God of Abraham, Isaac and Jacob. But as soon as they were away from our parents, they quickly do a 180 degree turnaround into their wicked ways. So, it seems my older half-brothers had come around to having faith in the Most High God after-all, but probably learning the hard way over the years.

As they talked among themselves and owned up about the wrongs they had done before while lifting up their eyes to God Almighty for mercy, I couldn't hold back the tears that were welling up in my own eyes from what I was being privy to. I quickly turned and moved away so that no one would start wondering why I was being emotionally moved by what these foreigners were saying - especially since they themselves still had no clue that I was their same brother who they had sold off years ago; or that I understood their vernacular as an interpreter was interpreting their conversations directed at me to me.

Chapter 12

The Power of Actions and Words

Actions Speak Louder than Words

Most of the time, our actions speak volumes and are a lot louder than the words coming out of our mouths. That's why it is written that we can tell or know what a person believes by what they do, or through their actions; and also that what a person thinks-on, will eventually become what they will do. So, I decided to see whether the 'professing-to-know-God' conversations of my older half-brothers would match their next line of chosen actions.

I set a plan off in motion to discover their true thoughts, motives and eventual actions, especially when 'nobody was watching'. By the way, there is no such thing as 'nobody is watching' because that is a lie of the trickster – the devil – because someone is usually watching in this days of technological advancement. Most important though is the fact that God is always watching, because He is the final Judge of all peoples.

According to my instructions, food was sold to the alleged 'spies', or my half-brothers (oblivious of our relationship still), but their monies were also hidden back into their sacks of grains – unknown to them. Also unknown to them was that it was not a mistake on our part, but a deliberate actions to see if they will come clean about what they might think we have no clue about. And so they set off on their journey back to their homeland.

They took off on their journey with such confidence that they would soon be back 'before we can say Jack Robinson' or faster than we could imagine, because they knew they were telling the truth about the last born child (named Benjamin) of their family of origin. They figured they would be able to return quickly with Benjamin as proof in order to free their other brother, Simeon, who was being held in detention. Truth always gives us unparalleled confidence that all will end well.

We however did not hear back from or see them return for a while, as they were very much unaware of my plan to unravel who they really were now; whether they were still their old self-centered and hypocritical selves, or now the new God-infused and selfless people that they professed with their mouths. They however finally showed up after their food supply had ran out and left them once again in the apparent danger of starvation.

When I saw them approaching from a long distance away, and that they had brought their youngest half-brother (my own only full-brother and only full-sibling), I gave instructions to my assistant to take them to my residence on their arrival. He was to settle them down based on further instructions I had given that will definitely 'put them on their toes' continuously as they wonder how I may be privy to further information about them that they would never expect anyone outside of their family of origin to know.

Guilt will tear You Up; Avoid What Leads to It!

When they arrived, my assistant proceeded to take them to my home, a mansion of great architectural design and a true masterpiece of astonishing intricacies that are weaved together in such a way that it will blow away the minds of even geniuses from other nations. When they discovered they had been taken to my mansion, they became even more alarmed.

Now, it wasn't immediately clear what was freaking them out, whether it was the architectural masterpiece of the front elevation of the mansion, or the elaborate security gadgets, or my top notch personnel that they had to go through to get inside, or simply the number of man hours that must have gone into the decorations on the inside, or the decorations themselves that just takes your breath away.

This is because they had not yet even gotten to the part where they were to be subtly introduced to the fact that I have more insider information about them than they could ever have imagined. The bewilderment on their faces just seemed to do a lot of the talking for them while they were still quietly taking everything-in in silent mode.

I had expected them to be excited about the nice way that they were being treated and for the fact that they were getting invited into the mansion of the official ruler of the most powerful nation of our time; but the opposite seemed to be the case. They had all gotten chatty among themselves again, brainstorming on what could be the reason why I had instructed for them to be taken directly to my mansion as soon as they arrived.

I overheard them saying one to another that they believe I was having them brought to my mansion so that I could overpower them and make them into my slaves. I then wondered how such a thought could ever come to their minds in light of the positive reception they were being afforded. Besides, a man of my standing doesn't need secrecy to do just anything he wanted (of-course, that would be actions without the fear of God).

Then it occurred to me that the guilt of what they had done several decades ago in selling their aspiring young half-brother into slavery was still gnawing badly at their heart with overwhelming power. And just because they dealt in slavery back then, they somehow believe everyone would be like them. They figured I would pay them back in kind and make them slaves as well.

As soon as they got an opportunity to speak though, they were all trying to explain the things that have happened from their last visit with us. This was their story that they presented to my assistant once they knew it was my mansion that they were about to enter:

'Dear sir, we know your Ruler is the great and powerful ruler of the greatest nation on earth – the only nation that not only has enough food to supply to her people, but also enough to supply to all nations at this most precarious time of global famine. Please be merciful to us and hear out the entirety of our explanation first'.

'We want you to know that we noticed that the monies we paid for the grains we came to buy the last time we were here, seemed to have made it back into the bags of grains sold to us one way or another. We were so terrified with the discovery that we just didn't know what to do for a very long time'.

'Who would ever believe a story like that – if just one person's money was found back in his grain sack, we can all agree that mistakes happen and call that a mistake; but for everyone's monies to have made it back into our respective grain bags was just going to be impossible to explain or believe'.

'But dear sir, if only you could kindly help us explain to the Ruler that we sure did not steal back our monies because there definitely was no way in the world we could have stolen from the most secure trading center in the whole world; we however made sure that we brought back all the monies that found their ways back into our bags, as well as new monies to buy more bags of grains'.

My assistant's reply seemed to have bewildered them the more as they asked one another whether these Egyptians were suddenly beginning to believe in the Most High God. My assistant told them that he believes their God, the God of their dad - The God of Abraham, Isaac and Jacob - must have put those monies into their bags of grains, since he (my assistant) knows for sure that he received their payments from them during that earlier visit'.

'So, chill (relax, be at peace) and enjoy your time here', he concluded in his reply to them. He also brought out Simeon from his detention and released him to be with them. I pray that the Most High will in His mercies and favor, cause people to put monies and whatever is needed into our lives where we were never expecting such, and even when we are being attacked by fear to expect the worst, in Jesus name.

A Time of Festivity or Mourning, Laughter or Sorrow?

And so these men from Canaan, my half-brothers (who still had no idea that I was their half-brother), now accompanied by my only full-brother, Benjamin, were brought in to my mansion and treated to royalty. They had house aids and assistants attending to them and their travel animals to help them get cleaned up, drink water and get ready for meal time with the Ruler of Egypt, all with live music and entertainment going on in the background for them.

They soon threw away their fears and inhibitions, and quickly adjusted to the fun and merriment going on around them and for them. They took in the sights from the writings and carvings on the walls, the detailed and 'out of this world' decorations and furnishings. And with the world class hospitality, they soon felt all at home. They also took cue from our orientation to details, and they decided to arrange the presents they brought in a most elegant fashion.

It is written in the Word of God that:
1. 'There is a time for everything ... a time to laugh and a time to mourn or cry ... a time to speak and a time to be quiet ... a time to embrace and a time to refrain'.
2. 'Teach us to apply Your (God's) wisdom to our lives'
3. 'It is better to go to a place of mourning than a place of laughter and feasting'; because that reminds us of the earthly initial end of all men/women and helps us to apply our hearts in wisdom.

The above sayings are different parts of scripture that are very important to take to heart, because, as human beings, we naturally want to be in a place of laughter, merriment, fun, feasting and celebration; especially when we are the ones being celebrated. And there is nothing wrong in celebration, except that most of those 'celebrations' are filled with people that have terrible thoughts and intents that are hidden underneath unreal laughter toward the people they are supposedly celebrating.

It is also written that a person may be someone who is thinking the opposite of what they are saying to you ... so he or she may say to you to please eat and drink, but in their heart, they do not want you to eat and drink; but if you go by the words of their mouth to eat and drink, then they will eventually make sure you pay dearly and regretfully for it.

If only these men had the idea of who I truly am (their young half-brother that they had forcibly sold off into slavery some decades ago), they would be terrified beyond their greatest phobias by the possibility of my likelihood to seek vengeance against them for the terrible and unspeakable things that I have had to go through as a result of their envy, jealousy and treachery over two decades earlier.

If only they had an idea of the elaborate plans and schemes I had set off in motion around them and targeted at them, they would be on their faces day and night crying out to the Almighty God for His mercy and help. If only they knew that they have been under constant surveillance since they approached our land the first time, and every minute they've spent here since then, and that they were constantly under a test, they would be very much alert and watchful of what they say and do - even in their vernacular.

But here they were, in the house of merriment, relaxed - just like my assistant told them to - and having a ball and the time of their lives. They nibbled on the hors d'oeuvre (appetizers) and sipped on the royal wines (non-alcoholic) and exclaimed that they never knew non-intoxicating wine could be this satisfying; and that the appetizers made their stomachs skip around in their bodies with untold excitement.

Then they were ushered into the main eating area in preparation for their meal with me at noon, with their faces flustering with unparalleled joy and pride in being treated as royalty most unexpectedly in this epicenter of the world. They however had no idea what kind of brouhaha (exciting trouble) they were in for over the next few hours as they sat down to prepare for my coming in.

As soon as I came in though, they all fell on their faces in greetings to me and also went on to present the different presents they had brought to me, one after another and in all reverence. I proceeded on to ask about their father whom they had made reference to the first time they came over. They replied that he was doing fine and that he sends his greetings and utmost respects.

Then I turned to the youngest and newest guy among them; 'is this your youngest brother that you all spoke of?' And they replied yes. I couldn't believe my eyes, as it has been tough keeping faith that this day would ever have materialized – a day when I stand right in front of my only living full sibling. I reached out and touched him to confirm that I was not dreaming, and said to him, 'God bless you my son'– He is much younger than I, just like I am much younger than my half-brothers.

Chapter 13

The Awesome One

Tears of Joy

When I touched Benjamin and looked into his face, I saw the resemblance between him and me - as I knew how I looked when I was younger, around his age now, and quite different from how I look now as a full blown Egyptian and the de facto Ruler of the nation. Unexpectedly and uncontrollably, tears started forming in my eyes, and I had to quickly turn away and rush off into my room to freely cry and weep.

 I couldn't stop crying in my room for a while as I reflected on the fact that the Most High God had truly been gracious and merciful to me in bringing my family of origin and myself together again - of course under the most unexpected and intriguing circumstances.

When people talk about tears of joy, it can be very strange to anyone who has not experienced it before. People usually cry when things that are negative or unpleasant happens to them, the people they love or care for, or just generally to people around them. This is where I truly come to the reality that God Almighty truly is awesome, and He alone is the true definition of Awesome.

But when things you have prayed for countlessly for days, turn to weeks and months, then years and finally decades, with it looking as if God was not listening, or is powerless to do anything about it, suddenly begin to be fulfilled right before your very own eyes, then tears of joy is definitely inevitable.

After a while, I was able to get a good grip of myself again, and I returned to the dining area to continue with everyone as they couldn't eat until I returned and gave the go ahead. As we sat down to eat, my assistants, chefs and servers set the table and seated each person present.

Racism is a Personal Choice

My Master Chef had me seated all by myself while all
my Egyptian officials were seated separately, and our
Jewish visitors from Canaan were also seated
separately. And you would want to ask us why the
separate seating as you would have thought we would
also seat at a large table or in small groups of tables in
very close proximity to make for easy conversation
making?

Well, the issue is that Egyptians (of my time)
considered it an abomination, a taboo or something
that must not be ever heard of, for them to seat at the
same table to eat with people of other nationalities
other than theirs. Before you start saying nasty things
about them having this superiority and better-than-
everyone else outlook and mentality, I have found that
such is common among other nationalities too.

Mankind's sin infused nature makes for different
nationalities, races, and ethnicities to tend
 towards the pride of life that makes us want to hold
our background, the nationality, race, ethnicity or
group that we now belong to, or have become a part of,
as superior to others. It is actually a good thing when
different nationalities get better and better at some
things over time than others, so long as they do not

belittle others, or worse still, attempt to destroy others or enslave them.

And as much as there may be national pride in our 'achievements', technological advancements, natural resources or agricultural and preservation advancements (as was our case), it is easy to lose sight of the fact that it is the Almighty God that has and does give us the resources, advancement or success. But He gives them to us so as to be a blessing to others and not a curse.

When a group of people are successful in any area of life and decide to use that to be of help to others (especially those who do not look or speak like them, or who come from other parts of the earth), then, they are being a huge blessing in the earth; but when they decide to push others down, and become 'Gods' over others in wickedness, then it is only a matter of time before the one and only true God Almighty humbles such a group or people.

The wonderful thing is that each person can and should decide to join in their national, race, ethnicity or group's ideology, practice or activities that help and lift up others, especially those different from them; but should shun, and choose to be different positively when it comes to evil, wicked, condescending and wrong ways of treating others.

Whatever nationality, race or ethnicity that you are from, know and come to terms with the fact that you are first an individual person, and each one of us will be judged before God Almighty as an individual person. Remember that you have choices and are able to make choices. Each one of us is also going to give an account to God about all the individual choices we made while on earth.

That age old excuse of the first man and woman - he/she/they made me do it - will not 'hold water', be tenable or be acceptable before God Almighty as the reason for doing the wrong things to others; whether they are different from us or not. Remember that this is a 'Dare Challenge Book'; *Dare* to be different positively, no matter the number of people who decide to be racist, superior-minded, mean, condescending, enslaving, belittling, bullying or even murdering others who are different from them or even alike them.

Take Note of Intriguing Things

An intriguing thing would be something that is out of the ordinary, or that catches our attention because it is unusual. It is always a good thing to take note of intriguing things, as there usually is something about it that is calling our attention to find out why something that is out of place, is really out of its normal place.

Our visitors from Canaan were seated according to their different ages, from the oldest, right down to the youngest, without our having asked for their ages. Now, this may look like 'what's the big deal in being able to tell who is older than who, especially among siblings'? If you take the time to look all around you and consider the siblings you know or have known over time, you will know that it is only when they are babies and toddlers that it is very apparent about who is older than who.

As siblings grow into adulthood, it is very common for each individual to have their unique growth that is not common to their other siblings. Many younger ones may grow a lot taller or more muscular or hefty; and it soon quickly becomes difficult to say who is older among grown up siblings.

The choice of clothes, hairstyles, wearing a beard and mustache or not, and personal carriage would also go a long way to shroud who is older than who among siblings. Needless to say was that this dumbfounding accuracy in seating them according to their ages freaked them out in no small way as we could clearly see the stupendous looks dotting their faces all across the room. They however were too terrified to bring themselves to asking how we knew the age position of each of the brothers, from the oldest right down to the youngest.

To cap it all up, I had the servers serve their youngest half-brother, Benjamin, with five (5) times more food than any of the other older brothers – even though it was very glaring that he was the very youngest because of the vast age difference, all of them were old enough to be his parents or even grandparents.

And it became flushed all over their faces again as they wondered why this 'small boy' called Benjamin was again being favored above the rest of them, his older half-brothers. This was supposed to bring back the old memories of favoritism that their dad played in favor of Joseph over the rest of them. We will see how they would respond to this favoritism in favor of Benjamin, if they would also think of how to get rid of him. They however also could not bring themselves to ask any questions about this capstone either.

If there was ever one thing I had learned over time, it is that God makes choices, especially when it comes to people, quite different from how we make our own choices. I have also come to understand that God's choices, especially when it comes to people, is far superior than ours, because God has access to all information about each one of us as individuals, that other people do not have access to.

He sees and knows what goes on in our hearts, even our motives, which are usually easily masqueraded to other people who believe that they know everything about other people close to them. Simply put, we decide or judge matters about other people based on what we see manifest on the outside, or that can be found out through our natural senses.

God, however, is able to see the hidden, untold, disguised and supernaturally-only-accessible things about us all. Many times, we tend to think that God is partial when He blesses some people or chooses them for special assignments; but God never does any of those without first knowing and then proving the hidden things of the heart of each person.

Conversations

Since, our visitors could not bring themselves to ask any questions on the things that were boggling and perplexing their hearts, they made do with the excitement of seeing their brother, Simeon alive again (they feared for his life). They basked in the euphoria of being reunited with him, eating, drinking, chatting and just simply enjoying themselves in the most prestigious environment they had ever been in. And chat-on they did.

They talked about how they and their very old dad had all discovered the monies they had paid for the grains they bought from us, back in their grain bags, back at home when they had opened their bags to get grains for food. They said they all felt paranoid and jinxed at the same time. They couldn't understand how each person's money had found its way back into the bags of grains that were sold to them.

They said they felt everything that could go wrong had gone wrong with them, and that they were sure to be accused of having stolen all the monies back. They all just assumed that Simeon was now also *lost*, as they couldn't see themselves coming back to Egypt, and credibly being able to explain how all their monies were back with them.

But to their utter dismay, the famine lingered on beyond that year again and they all soon ran out of food to eat. Then, they broached the subject of returning to Egypt to purchase more grain - of course having to take their youngest half-brother, Benjamin, along), with their father, and he didn't even want to hear any of it at all.

Somehow, they said their dad had chosen to blame the rest of them for the 'loss' of their other younger half-brother over two decades ago; because he said he had sent him out to go and search out his older half-siblings when they had not returned home in a long time from their business trip of the mobile arm of the family conglomerate. He insisted that he wouldn't have had to send Joseph out after us if we had only returned early as agreed.

'Our old man also blames us for not returning with Simeon back from our first visit here to buy food some time ago, when we were alleged to be spies, and were required to bring our youngest sibling as proof that we were telling the truth about not being spies. He kept saying that we were bereaving his old age with the loss of his children, one after another; first Joseph, then Simeon, and now we want to also take Benjamin away?, he had retorted'.

'So, how were you able to convince him to let you all come back with Benjamin', I asked them? Reuben said he then made his two sons into surety (guarantee, collateral) to their father, as he promised to bring Simeon back if he allows them to return to Egypt to buy food with Benjamin tagging along. He said he went as far as promising their dad that he could even kill his (Reuben's) two son's if he doesn't successfully bring Simeon back.

And I asked him what made him make such a bold move with their father when there was no guarantee that they would be able to bring Simeon back? He replied that they were all going to die anyway of hunger from the famine as their remaining food supply had ran dangerously low by that time. 'Wasn't that several months ago, why didn't you come then? I asked him further. "Because father still refused and was quite adamant to releasing Benjamin to go with us; he said a loss of Benjamin would definitely kill his already old and failing heart'.

Judah then chipped in that after several months of more waiting, they finally ran out of all food and starvation was gradually setting in again when he also approached their father and put his own self as surety for bringing Benjamin back alive. He said he also reasoned with their dad that if they do not take the risk of going to get more food with the lower probability of losing Benjamin and Simeon, then we face the sure reality of all of us dying of starvation - with all our families and his grandchildren inclusive.

'Our father finally gave in after a long time as he saw his grandchildren gradually loosing strength and vigor, with their lives slowly ebbing out in front of him. Father then asked us to pack the best of what we have from our land along with us as gifts to you, as well as to return the monies found in our bags and present new monies to buy more food on this next trip. He said he has come to terms with the fact that he may also lose Benjamin, but he at least will be able to save the rest of his extended family once we return with grain back from Egypt.'

'With that said, we quickly made preparation for the journey and set off almost immediately', Judah concluded. 'Wow! That was brave, self-sacrificial and touching of you guys to have offered your own selves and children as surety for the wellbeing of the other members of your large extended family, I exclaimed! 'I am extremely impressed at your dedication to the survival of others and your selflessness'; I said.

I watched their faces beaming with happiness that I was impressed with their efforts to save their families from starvation. We went on to enjoy the rest of the evening and talk some more over food, drinks (non-alcoholic) and entertainment. They were all beyond themselves how all their fears of what worse things could have happened to them at this second visit of theirs had rather turned out to be nothing but simply F.E.A.R. - False Evidence Appearing Real.

They had initially thought that no one would believe that they didn't steal their monies back from their first trip. They also feared that Simeon may have been tortured to reveal their 'plans' as spies, since the rest of them had failed to return back to Egypt a whole lot sooner with the evidence of their youngest sibling to prove otherwise; and he may have eventually been killed since he would have had no 'Spy plans' to divulge.

And finally, they had thought that the rest of them would have still been incarcerated and tortured to death, when they finally show-up. They were just never sure of what to expect of the 'Great Ruler' of the nation that had now definitely become the world's only superpower, from the fact that no other nation on earth had food. Also, everyone else had to come to Egypt to buy their food in order not to starve to death. But everything had rather turned out great for them in the end.

Chapter 14

Here Comes the Final Examination

Time for the Cap-Stone Test

As soon as it was daylight, the men were sent on their journey back to their starving families. New bags of grains had been loaded for them into their travel Extended or XL SUV's (animals), and they set off on their journey in high-spirits, overwhelming joy and excitement. Not only was Simeon returning home with them, but even Benjamin that their dad had feared the most for, that he would be lost like his only other full brother, was also going home with them.

And to cap it all up, they were carrying so much more food home to their starving families to ensure their survival through the rest of this unheard of kind of global famine that had threatened to wipe out all human existence; except for the saving grace of God having prepared the nation of Egypt to have preserved enough food, not for themselves, but also enough to feed the world.

But all their excitement soon came to a drastic halt, only a short way off into their journey back home. I had one of my assistants and some soldiers set off to pursue after them. They overtook the brothers a short distance off. He then laid the allegation at the feet of the brothers that they had stolen the Rulers 'diviners' silver cup, and wondered why they chose to repay all the good things their Ruler had done for them with this evil of stealing his diviner's cup - as if the cup can reveal any truth, not to talk of even tell the future.

The brothers quickly answered and spoke up in great confidence that they were very sure that none of them had taken the Rulers cup at any time. They displayed such great confidence that only comes from when a person is telling the truth, about not haven stolen the Ruler's cup. They seemed to have forgotten that one way or another that they couldn't explain, their monies already paid to buy grain had mysteriously found its way back into their grain bags earlier on.

Well, it does seemed like they didn't forget, because they actually brought up the incidence in their own defense. They quickly reminded my assistant about the fact that they had all found their monies paid to buy grain earlier on in their bags, but they had all returned the monies back to Egypt when they could have kept it without any of our officials being aware of it.

In their rash and unfounded confidence in their innocence, they even went on to say that if that cup was found with any of them, that person should be put to death, while the rest of them will willingly become the Ruler's slaves - such rash words. My servant then told them that their words will be used as the yardstick of judgement if the Ruler's cup was ever found on any of them.

The search got underway, and it was Deja-vu for the brothers rather quickly. The search began with the eldest brothers bags of grain, all the way down through to the youngest brother's bags. You needed to see the bewilderment on their faces as each person's bags began turning out the monies they had just paid for grains again the second time.

Each of them immediately tried to say that they were once again innocent on how the monies made it back into their bags, but they saw that that my servants seemed unmoved or unperturbed by the sight of those monies as they moved past them and kept searching for the Ruler's 'Diviners' Cup. The brother's faces seemed to sigh relief after it was not discovered in each of their bags right from the eldest to the very youngest?

'Wait a minute, what on earth is that?' exclaimed the brothers! 'Is that what we think it is – the Ruler's cup? How in the world did that get into Benjamin's bag of grains?' they all protested as the cup was gradually being pulled out of Benjamin's bag. The soldiers then surrounded Benjamin to signify that they were placing him under arrest.

Evidence of a Changed Heart

The rest of the brothers quickly loaded their SUV travel animals back up and followed their arrested brother back to my mansion. They all fell flat on their faces as soon as they got back to the mansion and appeared before me. I asked them why they did this horrible thing of stealing my 'divination' cup as if they had no idea that a man like me could easily find out hidden matters.

Then Judah spoke up from among them; he said there obviously was no way that they would be able to prove themselves innocent in this matter as the cup was found in their luggage – Benjamin's, to be precise. He went on to say that he believes the Lord was somehow exposing them to the wrongs they had committed before, and that they all have to become my servants now as a result.

I however refused their offer for every one of them to become my slaves for the 'wrongdoing' of only one of them - their youngest half-brother. I told them that the rest of them should go home to their respective families and their elderly father, because I fear God also, so that I do not punish the innocent along with the guilty.

Then Judah spoke up again and begged to have a word on the side or privately with me. He went on to narrate how he had made himself as the guarantor or surety with their father for their youngest brothers safe return home. I told him it was a shame that he promised to deliver what he had no control over, or certainty about; as he can see that I make the rules around here, but I do them with the fear of God in mind.

But Judah persisted very apologetically but firmly, that there was no way they can return home without their youngest brother as this will quickly lead to their father's untimely and sorrowful death. Benjamin seems to be the only reason keeping our elderly father alive because of a few reasons:

1. Benjamin is our Dad's second miracle child from the only wife and woman he ever loved, Rachael. Their mom had gone for so many years without having a child for our dad, such that everyone had given up hope that she would ever have children of her own. But God smiled on her much later in life as she gave birth to Joseph, and then much later on, to Benjamin as well.

2. Even though our father is married to four (4) wives, two official marriages, and two common law or concubine unofficial marriages, Benjamin's mom is really the only woman he freely chose to marry; the other wives became his wives and concubines outside of his own choice.

3. Since Joseph and Benjamin's mom, Rachael, was our dad's only wife of choice and love, it makes sense that he considers only Joseph and Benjamin as his true children of choice and love; even though he has ten other older male children and a daughter.

4. Joseph and Benjamin were each born to our dad in his old age when most people believed that he was done having children, and when most of the other wives had reached menopause and stopped giving birth. They were indirectly like grandchildren to him; or better put, they were like a combination of children and grandchildren into the same

individuals for him – 'child-grand', for lack of a better word.

5. Benjamin's only full brother, Joseph, had also gone missing several decades ago, with only his distinct 'coat of many colors' found afterwards, all torn up with blood all over it; which led us to believe that he must have been mauled by a wild animal.

6. To crown it all up, Joseph and Benjamin's mom, Rachael, had also died several years ago during her childbirth trauma, while giving birth to Benjamin, her second child. Her death had almost crippled their (also 'our') dad emotionally, with the only consolation that she had left the two children she had for our dad as living means for our him to constantly remember her by.

So, dear Ruler of the most powerful nation on earth, the reasons mentioned earlier are why we are not able to return to our elderly dad without the boy Benjamin. It would emotionally devastate our dad and send him to the grave in an untimely fashion and with the greatest of sorrows; please take me as your slave instead of Benjamin, Judah concluded.

Chapter 15

Meant to Blow Your Mind Away

Revelations: The Impossible(s)?

I could hardly believe that these were the same half-brothers of mine who were now exuding and demonstrating selflessness to the extent of standing as surety for their youngest half-brother, Benjamin, to our aged dad. But most impressive is the fact that they were even willing to become slaves instead of their youngest half-brother; even when all human evidence points to his being 'guilty' of the crime that he is accused of.

The 180 degree change and turn around in these much older half-brothers of ours was so great that I could hardly hold back the emotions coming over me, and the tears that soon started welling up in my eyes. 'Are these the same set of people who only thought of themselves and will do everything they can to get rid of everything and everyone that seem to be better off than they themselves, I asked myself'?

The revelation or realization that these erstwhile half-brothers that behaved more like racist's, household enemies, sell-outs, conspirators, get-rich-quick-and-dirty partners, slave peddlers, vision killers, healthy ambition antagonist's, cold-blooded killers, miserable counselors (people who hurt others and pretend to be consoling them) etc.; were now people who do not mind to lay down their own lives for the freedom and the wellbeing of an extended family member – especially one proved 'guilty'.

The revelation of the change of their hearts and characters was like the impossible happening before my very eyes. But as shocking as it was for me to learn of their new God-fearing hearts, what they were about to learn was either going to be on the same level as my discovery about them, or it was going to blow that out of the water for them.

I couldn't hold back my emotions anymore and as I was about to break down totally in tears, I ordered that all my officials should please leave the room. They hurriedly all rushed out and left me alone with this group of twelve foreigners, who until now, were alleged spies and a major threat to our nation.

As soon as we were left alone – the twelve 'spies' and I – I busted out crying and telling them that I was Joseph, the eleventh (11th) son in their family of origin. First, the looks on their faces turned deathly pale as if they had suffered from deadly allergic reactions to bee stings to their faces. They were first so shocked that I knew the name of Joseph and were still trying to figure out how I knew that name as the name of their eleventh half-brother.

Now the impossible(s) had just happened for them – Joseph, alive? And the Ruler of Egypt? Two revelations that stunned them beyond their wildest dreams and imaginations. 'Impossible!'; 'No, it can't be!'; 'Incredible!'; 'Someone please wake me out of this nightmare!'; 'No, I can't believe this!' were the different words coming out of their various mouths, and echoing all over the room.

I quickly moved forward with more undeniable deep knowledge that only they and Joseph -myself - could ever be privy to, and that no other human being on earth had ever known or had the secret revealed to them. 'I am Joseph, your baby half-brother, whom you sold off into slavery a few decades back for twenty pieces of silver. You did it because of your jealousy that quickly grew when you found out that I had great dreams, goals and ambitions to do great things in life.

'Is our dad still really alive, I asked them?' But none of them were able to answer me as I could see the look of terror written all over their faces. I could only imagine what kind of thoughts must have been racing through their minds – 'if this is truly Joseph still alive, then this is going to be our own day of death; because the natural human being would want to take revenge and kill us in return for our attempts at killing him decades ago and eventually selling him off into slavery'.

I however told them to come near me and see that it truly was I, Joseph, as I took off the head gear and mascara on my face that made me look mostly like an Egyptian, and never like a Canaanite immigrant. They came near me in desperate amazement, to verify for themselves whether it was truly I or not. They looked into my face and peeped at my eyes to determine whether it counters on satisfies their utter disbelief.

I however was crying out so loud and uncontrollably that my assistants and guards wanted to come back in to make sure that I was okay and that these foreigners or spies were not hurting me or overpowering me in any way; but I told them that I was okay and still needed to be alone with these people. They said that my cries were so loud that they could be heard as far away as Pharaoh's palace.

The Ways of God are Not the Ways of Mankind

I told them that they should not be afraid that I was not interested in taking any revenge against any of them. I told them that I had finally come to understand that it was God that had sent me ahead of them two decades ago in order to put me in a position to be able to provide for both the nation of Egypt and the rest of the world, at such a crucial time as this time of global famine and non-productivity.

I told them to listen to me very closely on what I was about to share with them:

1. I have come to understand that God's ways are completely different from the ways of the natural human being who is in the fallen nature of sin and servant hood to the evil one, Satan.
2. The ways of God are very much higher in wisdom, planning and strategies than the ways of mankind, even when God's ways seem foolish and does not

make sense; while the plans and strategies of the natural man may seem to make all the sense in the world, but they are never going to come close to God's ways and wisdom.

3. God will allow the enemy to carry out his worst plans and strategies against His children, yet God will use all the evil the enemy seems to have carried out for the good and fulfillment of His very best for His children.

4. God's timing is also completely different from the timing of the natural man. While man is very interested in 'faster and faster', God is more interested in 'better and best'. So, God's time may appear much more slower than man's ways, which is why He puts in and teaches us *patience*, a fruit of the Spirit that the world does not even want to hear about.

So, let me break it down to you or explain it in detail:

1. God is a righteous and Holy God and He wants His children to also be righteous and holy like He is, so that we can be reunited back with Him when we leave this world and live forever in His Kingdom of peace. Man's fallen nature is enslaved to Satan and evil or wicked ways, which are the opposite of God's ways.

2. While most of my mates as a teenager had a normal life of going through some kind of formal education, like going to 'elementary school through college', God took me through the 'school of slavery and incarceration', to prepare me for my life's purpose of saving enough food to save the world from being devastated by famine in the years to come.

3. And even though I would have preferred the 'normal' route my other mates went through, I realize now that my purpose was much more important to the saving of many nations, and I had to be well groomed to experience the lowest and the highest points of human living in order to be able to care for people at different levels of life and backgrounds.

4. The funny thing as I look back over my journey to the throne is that, even with all that the enemy (Satan) of my life, destiny, purpose, goals, plans and ambition had done to kill me and my dreams or ambitions (through attempted murder, slavery and jail time), he had only served to move me into God's very best position in life for me.

5. While you my older half-brothers had completely forgotten about me and believed that I should be long dead from the rigors and horrors of enslavement, God was allowing me to be moved closer and closer to my ultimate promotion and fulfillment.

6. Who would have thought it was wise for God to have allowed me to be sold off into slavery at the age of seventeen and then be lied against as having attempted the rape of my 'masters' wife, and then get thrown into the dungeons where I was supposed to rot away for the rest of my life? Wouldn't we think it was foolish of God to have allowed all such 'evils' to have happened to me? Yet, He was using it all to carry out the very best for me and even the people who had worked against me at different times.

7. Even though God's way of getting me to the top seemed skewed and awfully long in terms of timing – over twenty years – I am far better off for it today as He has made me Ruler of the most powerful nation in the world, and I get to do the honors of feeding the world in a time of crises as this one.

8. I have learned to literarily 'wait on God' while He carefully put the pieces of my life and times together, to make the ultimate beautiful picture of my life come to life and reality. Patience may be a fruit of the Spirit of God that we may naturally not be interested in, but it is a most important requirement that the Lord must bring us through in order to get to our very best in life. 'Waiting on God' literarily means we have to wait for Him to complete what He is doing in 'His own best time'.

9. Most of the time, we think we are ready for God's best, way too early before we really are ready to

handle His special weight of responsibilities for us. If you would have asked me, I thought I was ready to rule the world long ago at different stages of my life – when I was seventeen (17) and had the dreams of greatness; when I succeeded as a slave in the house of General Potiphar; when I succeeded in the dungeons and rose to the position of the chief Warden; when I interpreted the dreams of the Baker and Butler and their dreams happened as accurately as I had said; when the chief butler was being restored as the chief butler of the Pharaoh and I thought he would remember to put in a good word for me before the Pharaoh to secure my release; and the list goes on and on.

10. God will do far greater than we could ever imagine, dream about or plan on, when we rest in His all-encompassing wisdom, strength, ways and timings for our lives.

The Devil and his servants Work for God, Unconsciously

So, my dear brothers, while you believed you were doing much evil to me and destroying the dreams, goals and ambitions God had put in my heart and life,

God was actually working it out for my good, as well as your good, and the good of the whole world as well.

So, don't be afraid as I am not in the place of God to repay you for the wickedness that you had allowed the enemy (Satan) to use you to carry out against me - not knowing that God allowed the devil to move you all against me to get me to the very best place He had already determined ahead of time.

Most important to know is the reality that the famine the world as a whole was experiencing, that has lingered on for two (2) full years, and is about to enter into it's third (3rd) year, is not even half-way through its course or term; it will last for more than double the number of years it has lasted for so far.

As a matter of fact, it will be lasting for more than triple the number of years it has gone on for; because we still have five (5) more full years that there will be no agricultural growth anywhere in the world. And I know it sounds unbelievable and incredible, but this famine is running its seven (7) year course; just like the abundant years from which we were able to save all these grains that the nations of the world are coming to us to buy from, also lasted seven (7) years, exactly as God had told us.

This is why you must not beat yourself down over your past negative actions when you had attempted to kill me, and eventually sold me off into slavery. You have had a change of heart from such evil and wicked ways as I have been able to deduce from the tests I had put in place over your last two visits to Egypt.

I can testify that you all are changed men who now fear God and live selflessly in being willing to put your youngest half-brother's well-being ahead of yours; as well as consciously choosing to put yourself in enslavement rather than see our elderly father go down untimely into the grave from the avoidable 'loss' of your youngest half-brother.

Each one of us might have done terrible things in life that we are not proud of, or that we will do everything possible to keep hidden, so that others don't look at us as wicked and evil for the rest of our lives. But what is most important is to give our hearts to God in order for Him to give us a brand new heart – a heart that loves God fully first, and then loves other people to treat them well, just as we would want other people to treat us in life.

I can see how you treat your supposedly only remaining half-baby-brother, Benjamin, now, even though your dad (our dad) hasn't changed his playing the 'favoritism game' of putting the boy ahead of all of you his older half-brothers; and even counting the boy as if he were his 'only son', while he considers the rest of you as his 'children of circumstances' that he really doesn't directly count as his children of choice.

You do not let envy, jealousy or any form of hatred come into your hearts against Benjamin. Dad didn't quickly die off when I detained Simeon as he would definitely have done if you had all returned to him without Benjamin. You have allowed God to change your hearts even when the un-favored circumstances that surrounded you at home did not change.

And instead of blaming your dad, others or your circumstances for where you are today in life, you have taken charge of your lives to tow it after God's leadings and ways, as opposed to however you saw fit in order to get whatever you want in life - no matter whose ox is gored, or whoever is injured or done away with.

Quite crucial for you all, is also the fact that, though you were expecting revenge and retaliation against yourselves for the wrong and heinous acts you had done against me several years ago, God's ways however brings forgiveness, love, care, goodwill, provisions and protections, from me to you and your families.

God has made a former nobody like me to become a 'father' (most senior Advisor) to the foremost king over all the earth, the great Pharaoh of Egypt. How wondrous are the ways of God Almighty - He took a small and young boy, and made me the 'father' to an elderly Pharaoh. He took a foreigner and made me the foremost citizen of the most powerful nation on earth - a nation that considers people from my place of origin as an abomination, and only good for forced or slave labor.

The Most High God not only took a former slave of several years, but also a former 'convicted felon', and made me the law giver in the same nation where I had experienced the most difficult and unbearable years of my life. But most importantly for the nation of Egypt is that He has filled my heart with wisdom and grace to care for and provide for this nation at a most challenging time as this.

God is the Great Deliverer Who knew what the next set of decades held for us individually, as couples, families, groups, businesses, conglomerates, states and nations, and went ahead to get us prepared with the great savings plan He revealed to us to put in place to save us all from this years of failure of agricultural production that is now plaguing the whole world.

Chapter 16

I Miss You So Much, Daddy

Dear Daddy

Now, let us do this, you will take as much provision along with you back to get my (our) father and all your families - wives, children and grandchildren - as well as your flocks and herds and everything else that may belong to you; and bring them all back with you to live in the best part of Egypt, and close to me so that I can provide for you all from the abundance the good Lord has blessed us with.

Tell dad that his son, Joseph, said that God has made him Ruler over Egypt - the only nation with plenty at a time of global famine and un-productivity - please be quick to come over to me as I cannot wait to set me eyes on you again; because it was almost impossible to keep believing God that I would still see you again before you or I leave this world.

Tell dad that I know God told him it was Canaan that He was giving to him for his dynasty's inheritance; but that it is the same God who works in mysterious ways of making Egypt to be the only nation to have food on the earth at this time; and yet put that nation under my leadership, for the purpose of saving his dynasty and the world from starvation.

Tell dad that God reserves the right to determine how much of His plans He exposes us to, and even though this part was not initially revealed to him or any of us clearly, yet it was all part of His all-knowing plan. Come to think of it, God actually revealed this particular time in the future to us, we were the ones who didn't get a full understanding of it.

'Part of the dreams God had given to me several decades ago had shown the agricultural grains of my brothers falling to the ground all around mine, while mine remained upright; unfortunately everyone around at that time (including I) had interpreted it in terms of my brothers bowing down to me'.

'While in actually fact, it was pointing to the fact that grains and agriculture in other nations all around the world, except where I was, were going to fail or fall to the ground and be non-productive while the grains I was over would still be available for food - not growing at the time, but already earlier saved for the future time of the famine'.

'And the second dream had shown the sun, the moon and the eleven stars bowing down to me, which everyone had interpreted to mean, my earthly parents and eleven brothers would at some point be bowing down to me - and erroneous interpretation, as only God has the correct interpretation of the dreams He gives'.

'That dream however, as we can see from hindsight and after God had made it happen as He planned, was referring to the fact that the stars, sun and moon are seen all across the world, and that their bowing down to me actually represents that the nations of the world having been bowed down from the natural disaster of the famine, would all come to the nation of Egypt (under my leadership) for their food'.

'So, dear daddy, all roads from all across the world where you are, all point to and lead to Egypt at this crucial time of the world. Come to me as quickly as you can, as your dearest son is not only alive and well, but he is Ruler over all of Egypt, with enough to feed all nations of the world; especially you, and your dynasty'.

My brothers and I wept on one another for quite a while and talked in between our sobs also. I wept so hard over Benjamin and then over each of my other brothers - we all now refer to ourselves as full brothers, no longer half-brothers, considering how God had been merciful to us all, and brought us back together in spite of our earlier errors. Only God could have put us in this splendid position at such a challenging time as this.

Like Minds Think Alike

Word soon got to the Pharaoh that Joseph's brothers had come to Egypt. The Pharaoh and all his officials were very delighted and happy for me, as they knew how hard and lonely it had initially been for me over the years, and the fact that I had to forcefully make myself to forget about my background and family of origin; which I was likely not to have ever seen again, if not for the wondrous miracles and ways of the Most High God.

It is true that a person will attract those that are like minded, or that think like them, to themselves. I am very thankful to the Almighty God for the great Pharaoh whom He had put over such a great nation as this, for such a time as this, and especially for someone like me.

I know God specially picked this particular Pharaoh for me and for this special timing, because if it had been any other person, most people would have done very differently on a number of things that the Pharaoh did. Others would have out of the pride of life, continue to call themselves 'God' and would have refused the dreams, interpretations and directions that the Most High gave to this Pharaoh.

If it had also been someone else, that person, if a racist, would have been blinded to the fact that the Most High had put the solutions to the nation's biggest challenge, in the hands of a foreigner. He may also give every excuse of not putting me into leadership because of my past - I had been a slave and a convicted felon (outside my choice or volition).

But a mind that allows the Most High God into it will think like the Most High God. Such a mind is submitted to the Most High God, and so that mind will succeed at such most difficult times as this because it is dependent on the Most High, and not on itself, or the ordinary minds all around it that have the same background as it.

I am blessed with this Pharaoh because He has the mind of God, and because he submitted his natural mind to the infilling and leadership of the Almighty God. The same Spirit of the Most High that fills me heart and directs it, is the same Spirit that fill this Pharaoh's heart and also directs it. So we think alike and see things from the same perspective or point of view – the same point of view that the Most High sees from.

It is no wonder that the same thing I said to my brothers was what the Pharaoh reiterated and also spoke to me to tell them, even though no Egyptian had been in the room with me and my brothers when I had the discussion with them. Also, when we are good and kind to others, it becomes a lot easier for them to do likewise to us.

I am thankful that the Lord God had earlier used me to be forgiving to the people of Egypt, be kind and willing to offer a helping hand when God had put it only in my care, and to be a blessing to the Pharaoh and the whole nation of Egypt when I could have allowed the most base of human emotions – vengeance – and the difficult circumstances that had led me up to that moment and that still surrounded me at that moment, to dictate how to respond to them in their time of need; I would have sowed the wrong seeds for our future.

Now, the Pharaoh simply reciprocated the kindness and goodness the Lord had shown him and his people through me, when he said I should tell my brothers to take all the provisions they would need for a very comfortable journey back to Canaan; so as to bring all of their extended families and our elderly father to come and live in the best part of Canaan.

The Pharaoh also released the most comfortable limousines (wagons) to take along for the journey, so as to make it most comfortable and palatable. He had a custom made Maybach especially for our dad alone, to ensure his utmost comfort during the journey, considering his old age and health.

Then the Pharaoh said to tell them to only return with things that they considered indispensable either because of their beliefs or anything else. He said to let them know that the very best of the nation of Egypt was now theirs – the lands, technology, comfort and goodness that all other nations had brought into Egypt in order to buy food.

'They shouldn't bother bringing their regular belongings from Canaan as they will never lack any good thing anymore'; the Pharaoh finalized his instructions to me. I thanked the Pharaoh and went on to get my brothers prepared for their journey back to what they had called home for decades, Canaan, and to return back to their very new home nation, the great land of Egypt.

Errors of the Fathers (or Mothers) Showing up in the Sons (or Daughters)

My people look at me and think that my life was without any faults, and that I was kind of like the perfect person. After all the hatred, animosity and terrible situations I had gone through, for me to have forgiven my brothers from my family of origin, and my other 'brothers' – the people of Egypt – makes people look at me as spotless.

But I did have my struggles at each and every point in time and especially at different points that were major landmarks in my life's journey. But in preparing my brothers for their journey, I noticed I had also consciously or unconsciously done one of the things we had all considered a major error or flaw that was common to my dad – playing favorites.

It is noteworthy because our dad, Jacob, had said that playing favorites was a major error or fault in his own father's (Isaac's) life also. More alarming is the fact that dad said it was evident in his own grandfathers (Abraham's) life also. What probably made it pass from one generation to another seems to be the fact that none of the generational fathers had acknowledged it as an error that had caused so much harm; and so none of them had confronted it.

But I saw that I soon played favoritism with Benjamin a second time during this second visit of my other brothers, but Benjamin's first visit to Egypt. I made provisions available to them all for their journey, and then saw that I had intentionally given five (5) times what I had given to each of my other brothers, to Benjamin. Not only that, I had also given him so much money to carry along than he and they all must have seen in their lives so far.

And looking back in retrospect, I had also done a similar thing when they had all been brought to my mansion for lunch with me when they initially arrived with Benjamin on this particular trip to Egypt. I remember that I had given five (5) times the amount of food that I had given to each of my other brothers, to Benjamin.

You might say to yourself, what is wrong in being extra kind to whoever I choose to over others? And why can't I distinguish my own full-brother/sister from my half-brothers/sisters with what I choose to give him or her? There shouldn't be anything wrong in my showing preference and favoritism to a person of my choice even if they have not done anything extra over others.

On the surface of things, there seems to be nothing wrong in any of us showing favoritism toward anyone of our choice. The issue is that, such acts of favoritism usually provoke feeling of unjust treatment to others who see the unfair advantage given to someone else, especially when the person is less qualified or naturally hasn't done anything extra to warrant it.

There are countless examples I have to buttress this. But first, I have to commend my other brothers who have had their hearts infused with the presence of the Spirit of God such that they had not allowed my acts of favoritism to Benjamin to raise another set of ugly feelings of animosity and hatred.

I remember that dad, Jacob (Israel) had told us how our own great grandad and his own grandad, Abraham, with his wife, great-grandma Sarah, had on their own volition, accord and choice, made their maid to have a child (Ishmael) for them when they could not have a child for decades, but had soon quickly turned around to play favoritism with their own biological child, grandpa Isaac, once he came along.

They not only treated Ishmael differently, but soon considered him as a mistake and as an illegitimate child, to the extent of sending him and his mom away from them, and not caring whatever happened to them afterwards. Whether they died or not, were provided for or not, didn't seem to have bothered Abraham and Sarah anymore.

They had simply used the maid Sarah and her son Ishmael, and then dumped them once they felt that they no longer had any more use for them. Their favoritism at that time still seem to be plaguing the whole world centuries later with all forms of hatred and animosity between those two children that actually came from the same father but different mothers.

And then we move on down from Great-grandpa Abraham, to grandpa Isaac and his wife, grandma Rebekah, who maintained a monogamous marriage relationship throughout their lives. You would have expected that they would have gotten away with the feeling of the need to play favoritism as there were no 'extra-wives' or concubines, or half or full siblings to polarize them.

Grandpa Isaac and Grandma Rebekah even had twins as their children, born on the same day and almost at the same time, from the same father and mother; yet, each of the parents soon quickly chose favorites among their twin sons and helped to develop their individual lives into a lifetime of hatred, betrayal, cheating, and trickeries, that had them only one step away from murdering each other at different times.

My two earlier books covers the unbelievable challenges that came as a result of those seemingly harmless lifestyles of favoritism that our great-grandparents and later grandparents exhibited and considered harmless. The books are:

1. Who Am I? Going Rogue: Discover and Become the Best You!
2. Who Am I? Big Dreams: Never Say Never to Your Dreams and Ambitions!

Both books by Dare Adebiyi (BenKing)

And last, but not the least, we look at the favoritism that our dad, Jacob (Israel) had played out before our eyes as we grew up and how that only led to unbelievable acts of envy, jealousy, hatred, betrayal, attempted murders, selling off into slavery, unimaginable loneliness and hardships; as covered in this 3rd book 'Who Am I? Trillionaire's Saga: Attain and Maximize your Trillions.

So, you see why I have to come to terms with the reality of the destruction that playing favoritism brings among those that should be one another's family members, groups, business associates, company workers or officials, different nations and the world in general. I have to confront this issue and lay it on the altar of God Almighty for His help, deliverance and constant reminder to avoid it like the destructive plague it is.

Therefore I cry out in prayers to the Surgeon of surgeons, the One Whose Word is able to get to the invisible but most important parts of a human being – the Soul and the Spirit – and to uproot evil plantings of favoritism that disguises itself as harmless; to please uproot every evil planting's in my heart and dynasty today, and to destroy it, so that I may treat everyone. fairly and without the evil of favoritism, in Jesus name. I suggest you pray that prayer for yourself too, and for your dynasty as well.

Chapter 17

Change of heart (Relocation): Going Places...

In Order to Go Places

Sometimes, we think we're done with all that we came to do in this life. We may feel we have done it all, seen it all and are totally convinced that our life's purposes have been fulfilled. We might even be very old and so frail, that we might just be taking it so easy because any strenuous activity or long journey would put us over the edge and out of this life.

But when God say's it's not yet over for you, then it surely is not yet over. Even if the whole world say's it is over for you - your company, boss, friends, family, spouse, parents, children, doctor, judge, financial institution, credit bureau or your nation – if God says you are still going places, then you definitely are.

My dad, Jacob (Israel), I am sure would naturally not want to make the long journey all the way from Canaan to Egypt. I'm sure he would say that there was absolutely no reason in the world for him to make that journey, and there never will be any reason strong enough to make him do it. Taking a trip to Egypt will already be unacceptable enough, but relocating there would even be considered an abomination to him.

I'm sure he would give several cogent and tenable reasons why he should not, and will not take a trip to Egypt, not to talk of relocate to live here. He would say:

1. Egypt is a pagan nation where they even treat their king as 'God' and he will not have anything to do with such a place.
2. God had promised his own grandfather (Abraham) and his own father (Isaac) the land of Canaan as their inheritance and had never spoken of ever living in Egypt; so he naturally believes *this is outside God's will for their dynasty.*
3. He senses this trip to be a trap to get the whole of their dynasty to come to Egypt and then enslaved or imprisoned as the last trip led to exactly that for his son Simeon.

4. Besides, in his present stage of health, such a long trip will be too much for him and would only lead to his demise or death on the way.
5. Finally, even if he has to die of hunger in Canaan, then he would rather do that as he is old enough to die, and he has already seen his children's children.

What my dad was about to find out however was that God had not finished with him yet. He had believed he was likely going to *die in sorrow from the loss* of his special wife (Rachael), most special child (Joseph), second special child (Benjamin) and then each of his other regular children - starting with Simeon who was already detained in Egypt and whom they were not even sure if he was still alive.

What daddy Jacob was about to find out would blow his mind away and rejuvenate his life all over again like never before. He was about to find out that I was alive and the Ruler of the most powerful nation on earth, and the only nation that has enough food to feed the rest of the world; namely Egypt the Great.

Not only will he have the opportunity to be reunited with me, but he was also going to meet my wife and the grandchildren he never knew he had from his most special son. He is also about to find out that neither himself, nor any of his children and grandchildren that he had been watching slowly fading away into death from starvation, would be dying of starvation anymore; they all however will be well fed, nourished and taken care of with the best there is in the whole world.

But for God to change anyone's story from worst to best, starvation to plenty, sorrow to joy, loses to recovery, dying to living well, poverty to wealth, failure to success, barrenness to fruitfulness etc., we must be willing to follow God's directives even when they seem foolish or impracticable.

We must be willing to move when God says to move. First, what is God saying to you to do that you may think is way beyond you? We have to first relocate our hearts or beliefs from what and where we are, to what and where God wants us. Simply put, we much be willing to change our minds when God say's so and agree with what He tells us.

And even if he wants us to physically relocate, then we must be willing to. Relocating simply means a change – change of job, skills, industry, those around us, environment, city, state, nation or even continent. For the sad story of my dad and his dynasty to change for the best, they would all have to change their current mindset and physical location from Canaan to Egypt at this point in time in their lives.

Your story and life are not over until God says so. This has been evidenced throughout the several generations of our dynasty over the years. First, my great-grandparents were told they would never have their own biological children, but they eventually did at 90 years of age for great-grandma, and 100 years of age for great-grandpa.

Afterwards, my grandparents, Isaac and Rebekah also experienced prolonged delay before having their own children. The same held true for my dad and mom, Jacob and Rachael. Even though the other wives of my dad were all having children for him without any stress or delays, my mom did not have any child for way too many years and everyone simply gave up hope for her.

And because God was not done with my mom, she eventually gave birth to me, and my dad became super attached to me as he named me his miracle child of his old age. After having me, my mom continued to make concerted and tremendous efforts to have more children unsuccessfully. People again thought it was over for her and that she would end her life with only one child, me.

God then proved everyone wrong again about my mom as she eventually gave birth to another child before she died, and that was my baby brother Benjamin. My mother's story and life was not over in the barren and

non-productive stage, as most people had thought.
God took her past the unproductive years to eventually
give birth to my brother and I - who later literarily
became the Ruler of the world and its food provider.

Then, the same God who told great-Grandpa Abraham
not to be like the people who lived around him in
Canaan who usually and often kill their children as
sacrifices to idols, was the same God who later tested
him by requesting for him to kill as a sacrifice, the only
child of promise He had given him in his old age.

But because Abraham was willing to relocate (change)
his mind into what God was now saying, and went
three days journey to get to the location where he was
supposed to carry out the instruction; God stopped him
from killing the child in the nick of time, and provided
a ram to be killed for the sacrifice instead. God then
swore to Abraham that because he had relocated
(changed) his mind to obey Him, He was going to bless
the whole world through his dynasty.

I, Joseph, am part of that dynasty that God said would
be the channel He would use to bless the whole world.
The whole world is now coming in to the nation I lead,
Egypt, for their food and livelihood. *In order to go to
places in life, we may literarily have to go to places we
never planned for or imagined.*

I tremble at the thought of what would have happened if great-grandpa Abraham had refused to relocate or change his mind in order to obey God, or if he had told wife about God's instruction and let her be responsible for fighting him to a stand-off or stand-down on it, or if he had simply refused to give that most precious gift of his son in the person of grandpa Isaac, as requested by God?

Sometimes, God just wants to see if we would be willing to trust Him and change our minds in order to obey Him on something we would never have bulged about. He wants to see if our obedience to Him will be complete and if we will be willing to go to places untold of, or abominable to us, as long as He is the One leading - even though He may later stop us from that abominable just in the nick of time.

I however made sure that I sent enough things with my brothers back to Canaan that would convince my dad that I was truly alive and the Ruler of Egypt. Except if his son's had gone on to pull off the biggest heist or robbery of the century - like successfully robbing the Central Bank of Egypt - in which case, they would all be long dead before even making it in, not to talk of making it out, then there was no way they would have gotten the things they took back to convince my dad.

I know my dad, daddy Jacob, was a man of faith, however, the much I know of him had also taught me while I was growing up around him, that his own kind of 'faith' had to see, touch and feel in order to believe. You could say his own kind of 'faith' believes in checking things out, or confirming everything, or testing things, or simply just making sure that no one was deceiving him or 'taking him for a ride'.

I had his name inscribed on the hand-sewn supple leather seats of the Maybach ride and a custom made license plate that also fully spelled out his God-given new name. He must know that there was no way his boys must have been able to lay their hands on such technologically-advanced custom made ride with his name etched into it without the realization that this must have come from the richest and most powerful man in the world - and that must be his very own son, Joseph. I made sure that the back seats could recline enough into a lying down position to make sure that he could be most comfortable and never stressed during the journey.

Atta boy - No Quarrels Please

As the guys set-off on their journey back to Canaan, I called out to them to have a parting conversation with them; 'Atta boy' - Way to go, guys! This is truly a day that the Lord God has made and we must rejoice and be thankful about it. I know that the thoughts of regret for the wrong things you did decades ago would resurface at different times on the way in order to distract you and cause blame-game quarrels, please don't give in to it.

But, seriously please, there is absolutely no need to give in to that temptation of quarreling with, or blaming one another on the way. You know I heard you guys viciously engage in that blaming game while you were under my scrutiny and you had not known then that I was your brother Joseph; that is over-with now.

Don't allow guilt to tear you up individually or apart as brothers. You have every reason in the world to be happy and thankful all the way home and back here. Let's go over those reasons together:

1. The guilt you had carried for decades that you must have indirectly had me killed during my enslavement, has been overturned as you've discovered that I am not dead, but alive.
2. Your guilt and heartache would have been greatly multiplied if you had mistakenly come across me in Egypt still a slave in hard grueling labors; and of course there would have been nothing you would have been able to do to get me out of it. A slave in

most place is usually kept as a slave for the rest of his or her life.

3. If you all had not had a change of heart or allowed God to relocate your hearts from the wicked and evil control of Satan, to His own loving leadership, I would have kept only my full brother, Benjamin, back here with me in order to deliver him from going through wickedness at your hands, just like I had gone through. Then, you would have had to go back to face dad without Benjamin, and watch him quickly die of sorrow; the sorrow that would have eventually eaten all of you up too.

4. What if I had also not had a relocation of heart, from satanic vengeance, to the forgiving heart that God gives, and I had rather pursued vengeance against you all - including your wives, children and grandchildren? If I had submitted to the satanic heart, I would have made you and your generations' slaves, and tortured you all daily for decades to try and satisfy the decades of suffering I had to go through as a result of your initial wickedness against me.

5. Just a few weeks ago, our father's family dynasty faced starvation and starred at extinction right in the face with no hope of making it through. This was because the only nation (Egypt), that had food, had chosen to be hostile to y'all, for reasons unknown to y'all, and which you couldn't fathom; while it was selling food to everyone else. But now,

those reasons have not only been exposed to you, but also overturned in your favor.

6. Besides, strife destroys and robs of good things, while peace ensures a fertile ground for great things to grow and develop in.

7. Finally, dwelling on the errors and failures of the past will only rob you of the joys, provisions, successes, peace, victories, opportunities and glories of today and tomorrow.

Sometimes, success, victories, plenty, and breakthroughs are more difficult for many people to handle. Sometimes, dysfunction, lack, poverty and failures are more comfortable and easier for some people to handle, as there is nothing to get greedy about or kill for. I am sure that you all are already well equipped with a relocated or changed heart to handle this great success the God Lord has brought us all into. Go and get daddy and your families please. Adios!

He's Alive? Who? Say Again? No Way!

So, off they went back to Canaan, to our dad and their families. And they did well not to have quarreled on the way as that would have polluted their extravagant joy that radiated all over them and that made their 'bombshell' kind of news easier to digest. Strife would definitely have polluted their great news and watered it down into nothingness – because, if they truly brought great news, why quarrel instead of celebrate?

As they approached home, their celebration and jubilation could be heard from some distance away. And so everyone around were curious about what all the boisterous noise was about, as most people in the neighborhood were frail and worn out from lack of good nutrition over an extensive period of time that the famine had brought about.

He's alive! He's alive! Joseph is alive! Joseph is alive! Who? Who is alive? Say again? Come again? Sorry, I didn't hear you well, Joe is alive? Joe who? Joe J.? Joe Jake? Who on earth is Joe Jake? Joseph? Which Joseph? Son of who? Who is the dad? Who is the mom? No way! Impossible! It cannot be! It must be a ghost! Incredible! If he is alive, where has he been all these years? Isn't that the kid that disappeared decades ago? Wasn't he reportedly killed by a wild animal? If he wasn't killed then, did he run away from home? The tumultuous questions were all over the neighborhood.

But the joyous exclamation from my brothers soon filled the whole place and echoed well ahead of them, getting to my dad also. The guys ran into our huge extended family compound of houses and headed straight for dad's in the center. But dad was already on his feet and struggling to get out into the yard to meet them.

'Daddy, Baba, Papa, Joseph is alive! Praise God Almighty! Your son Joseph is alive and well!' the guys kept saying. 'Impossible! No way', dad muttered! 'I order you to stop playing this terrible and not-funny prank on me', dad roared at them. 'Which Joseph are you all talking about, because my son Joseph was killed by a wild animal decades ago', their dad queried them.

'Your very own Joseph, your very special miracle first born son of your dearest and most special wife, Rachael. The older brother of your only other special child, Benjamin; and yes, the one everyone believed had been killed by a wild animal decades ago, he is the one we are referring to'; they answered.

'I have dealt with the loss of my most precious son over two decades ago and do not want anyone reminding me about it, let alone, giving me false hope of him being alive', dad struggled to bring the words out of his strained breath. 'Stop being cruel to me with this unfounded and untrue news you are peddling; my weakened heart is not able to take this anymore', he pleaded with them.

'But daddy, it's true, and you haven't even heard the more incredible part of it all – Joseph is the Ruler of all of Egypt! Baba, Joseph is the second most powerful man on earth; practically the most powerful man on earth'; they continued. 'The king of Egypt is the ceremonial head of Egypt, but Joseph is the Official head of Egypt, daddy, can you believe that?' they rhetorically asked him.

'Papa, Joseph is not just practically the most powerful man on earth, he also is practically the richest man on earth; all the food resource in Egypt that all nations are heading there to buy from, are under his control. Joseph practically is the one feeding all peoples and nations of the earth at this period of global famine', they insisted.

'Since all of the things we have said still do not convince you, dad, then, your son, Joseph seems to know you all too well, notwithstanding the fact that he has not seen you for decades. Funny that he said you were not likely to buy our stories until we present further evidences that he made available to us.' He has sent someone, and several things to convince you.'

'First, here is Simeon back, well and alive, even though we couldn't vouch if he had been kept alive after we didn't return back to Egypt to corroborate the information we gave them on our first trip there. If you want to, you can say you have practically received Simeon back from the dead also; though he was never killed over there, just as Joseph was never killed.'

'Next in the evidence line-up, are the finer things of life that your son Joseph knows you like and have a flare for, just like he also does like such things; you know that he really took after you on such. He said he knows how you like custom made things, as it depicts your individuality and unique perceptions.'

'Baba, take a look at the most technologically advanced vehicle you or any of us have ever seen. It is called the Maybach. But this is not just any Maybach, it's got your God-given name etched into the seats, the license plates, the hood and the rear of the car. Remember how you and Joseph did all your own little bitty customizations on the Ferrari car (coat of many colors) you had gotten him back in time?'

'Even if we had wished and attempted to steal this car after all such customizations had been done to it at an insane cost, we wouldn't have been able to come out alive out of the superpower nation of Egypt. And look at all the other luxurious things Joseph has sent you with your name etched on each one of them; Tell us, daddy, are you still in doubt?'

Jacob took his time to go through everything that had been brought back from Egypt to him, supposedly from his 'long dead' son, Joseph. He ran his hands over the etchings of his name on the outside and the inside of the wagon (Maybach);and then moved on to the other handcrafted luxurious items and gadgets that were specifically made for him showing his name imprinted, stitched, carved or etched into them. Then the seemingly impossible happened: Our dearest father exclaimed:

'My Son is alive! My Joseph is alive! My son of miracle is alive! The son of my heartthrob is alive! The memory of my dear Rachael lives on through my dear son Joseph! My son Joseph is literarily back from the dead. I have known him as being dead for over twenty years (20) now, but he's back! Glory! Hallelujah! This is perhaps the happiest day of my life! Joseph is alive and I must go to see him before I die; I am ready, let's go!

Chapter 18

Leaps of Faith for New Beginnings

Journeys into the Known Unknown

My dad, Jacob, was about to embark on a journey into what can be said to be both the known and the unknown. It appears to be known because everyone and everything around him say so - that he was going to meet his erstwhile long dead, but now resurrected (or simply never dead) son, Joseph. And that son of his happens to be the Ruler in a foreign nation, that just so happens to be the foremost world superpower.

The journey however, appears to be unknown because there are no guarantees that what everyone and everything around him say about Joseph being alive and being the ruler of the foremost nation in the world, may prove true. How can he know that he is not just taking all of his generations into a trap of permanent enslavement and eventual extinction?

But our God is the One that closes a door that He Himself had earlier opened to us, when the time comes when He opens another door that He wants us to go through. The Most High has ordained or prepared our times, seasons and locations while on earth, well ahead of our births, and He will guide us into them at each appropriate time and setting.

Even though He was the One who had opened the door of Canaan to our Great-Grandad, Father Abraham, several decades prior when He asked Abraham to move or physically relocate to a land that He would be showing him. Abraham made that journey in faith without all the full details given to him.

Abraham moved away from all the people he had ever known and relations in the nation called Hur of the Chaldeans, when God called him out from there and closed the door of that land to him. God promised to take him to a land that he and his generations after can call their own land, home and nation, while the earth remains.

Abraham and the next two generations after him (Grandpa Isaac and now our dad, Jacob), have been living in the new door or land of Canaan that the Lord

God had opened to them for decades now; and even dad's own children have had children that lived in Canaan. But it does seem that God was closing the door of Canaan to our generations for now, and opening the door of Egypt, also for now.

And so the leap of faith was taken in embarking on the journey to Egypt - our new door and nation - from Canaan - our old door and nation. No food has grown in any nation on the surface of the earth over the last two years; and that does include Canaan and even Egypt. Yet, Egypt is the only nation on earth with food for its people and extra food to sell to other nations of the world.

Yet, most crucial of all pointers as to what door or nation is open to us or closed to us, is the fact that Joseph, the great-grandson of Abraham (our founding patriarch), is the Ruler of the only nation where there is food for the whole world at a time of global agricultural and growth failure. And the whole process that God worked through to make that happen was simply beyond anyone's anticipation or comprehension.

Sometimes, the realities that surround the doors in front and behind us, are what God will use as pointers to which door He has closed and which one He has opened. At such times, we may not hear God expressly say to us that this is a door I have closed, and that is the door I have opened. Sometimes, the things in creation themselves echo the voice and will of God in themselves.

So, daddy started out on the journey without a clear instruction from God, but with all the things mentioned earlier as pointers to the fact that God seems to have opened the door of Egypt by sending Joseph there in the most unorthodox way, and taking him to the very top of leadership there in even a most incredible and miraculous way.

As they journeyed toward Egypt though, they soon came across Beersheba - a place that holds a lot of history right from the first patriarch of our dynasty, great-grandpa Abraham, right through to daddy Jacob himself. It was in Beersheba that great-grandpa Abraham got a peace accord signed with King Abimelech when their workers clashed over wells dug and their ingenuous irrigation systems.

Grandpa Isaac also had a major experience and encounter in Beersheba. The Lord also visited him there during a period of famine, and after his servants had gone through many conflicts over the wells they had dug, which other people had struggled against them to take. Funny how some battles that have been won by a generation, also show up in the next generation for a rematch.

And, last but not least, was that even daddy Jacob had also had a special encounter with the Lord while he traveled away from his twin brother, Esau's deathly anger and promised revenge for Dad having conned him out of both his birth right and the final blessings that the father was supposed to have given to him as the original first born. Of course, daddy had not told his twin brother that he was relocation away from him, but had gone away under the guise that he was obeying his parents in going to marry from his mother's family of origin as they had requested.

Encountering God Personally

In daddy's travel though, he had just left Beersheba when he retired for the night and had a dream where he saw a ladder reaching into heaven with angels going up and down on the ladder. He also saw the Lord God standing at the top and pronouncing blessings on him, by assuring him of generational multiplications, protection, and blessings that will overflow in his life to bless all peoples of the earth.

When my dad - Jacob had woken up from that dream, he had honored the Lord in that place by building an alter with the stone he had used as a pillow for the night. He had poured oil on the rock and promised that if God did all that He had promised him - remember that daddy loves to see it happen first - then the Lord God will be his God and he will in return also give a tenth of all the blessings back as an offering to God.

Dad had also called the name of that place Bethel - the House of God, the Gateway to Heaven or simply a very Great Place. The name of the place was originally called Luz, but daddy's experience with God changed that to him personally. Dad's renaming that location based on his experience with God, was one of the lessons he had shared with us when we were much younger.

Daddy had pointed out that a place or thing may mean several different things to several different individuals or groups, based on their individual or group experiences. Even within a group, each person may also come away with individual experiences that differ from others within the same group or the same encounter. This is why we all must experience God individually, and have a personal or individual relationship with Him.

Each person has to take their individual leaps of faith to respond positively to the Lord God, whenever He comes looking for us as he did with each of Great-grandpa Abraham, Grandpa Isaac and Daddy Jacob. Each of their encounters with God were different, but all of the encounters were geared toward the same thing – having a personal and individual relationship with God.

And each person will have that encounter at one point or the other where the Lord God reaches out to have a relationship with you. Jesus said that He stands at the door of each person's heart, knocking, and that anyone who opens his or her heart to Him in faith, will experience the fellowship, friendship, leadership and salvation that He, the Father and Spirit will bring to such a person's life.

Will you open the door of your heart to them today? Wherever you may be at this moment, simply ask Jesus to come into your heart and be your savior; also ask Him to be your leader and Lord from now on, so that He can make sure that it is well with you throughout the rest of your earthly stay. He will also ensure that you can be at peace, joy, and fulfillment forever and ever with Him in His Kingdom whenever you leave this earth. Do it now, pray that simple prayer and don't dare put it off.

Returning to God

Our daddy, Jacob, on his way to Egypt with all of his extended families, first made a stop at Beersheba - the place where his grandfather and father had experienced God - to fellowship with God and see what the Lord will say to him about this journey. His dynasty was on the line with this move and it was important to him to make sure he was on the right path.

As much as everything points to this relocation being Gods will and plan for Jacob and all his descendants, It was very commendable that dad still put all his excitement aside to seek Gods mind on this major step that seems to contradict everything else that God had earlier said to him and his ancestors - that Canaan was His place of settlement for them.

Dad returned to his fellowship with God and offered sacrifices in Beersheba. He spent time in communion with the Lord and honored God again. He revamped and re-ignited his faith in the Lord, as the Lord had shown him that it was not over for him nor his dynasty. Even though his faith had been sorely challenged over the years, he made a conscious choice of returning to the Lord in response to God's miraculous intervention in the famine that would have wiped away our generations for good.

Daddy had gone through many challenges over the years that seemed to have made his fellowship with the Lord to grow cold. He had experienced the challenge of barrenness from the wife he loved, Rachael, not being able to have a child for a very long time while everyone else around her, including her own older sister, Leah, and both of the maids, were having children with ease.

Of course, mom – Rachael – later gave birth to myself and later Benjamin. But it was most heart wrenching that as soon as that challenge of barrenness was going away, it was replaced by an even greater challenge of our mom dying during her time of giving birth to my brother, Benjamin.

Daddy's loss of the wife he loved very much was a most devastating blow to his faith. He had mourned her passing so much that everyone around him thought he was not going to last long afterward. But dad took comfort in the fact that his loved wife, Rachael, had left him with two wonderful children that could always serve as reminders to him about her.

While he was being comforted with having the two sons of Rachael as comfort to him, disaster soon struck again when I went missing over twenty years ago. All his prayers that I would return back home safely seemed to have gone unanswered when my older half-brothers had returned with my Coat of Many Colors (Ferrari with custom paint job) that was torn all over and drenched in blood – a pointer to my demise or death.

My 'demise' seemed to have been the 'last straw that broke the camel's back' in my dad's faith. He just seemed to have grown lukewarm toward God after that. God seemed to have been 'failing' him at different and crucial periods in his life and he seemed to have just barely hung on to his faith.

But those were just some of the challenges that rocked dad's faith from my mom's side of the family. Other challenges had showed up at different times from the other wives sides of the family. Dad's daughter, Dinah, from his first wife, Leah, had gone out to be with the women of the city and had ended up getting raped by the son of the governor of that city.

As if the rape was not enough of a challenge, Shechem, the guy who raped her then proposed marriage to her. Dinah's brothers, Simeon and Levi, however hatched a plan of revenge in which they pretended that they welcomed the marriage proposal from Shechem, but required all the men of their city to become circumcised before the marriage.

The brothers then capitalized on the immobilizing effect of the circumcision surgery to kill all the males of that city. That mass slaughter soon left all of dad's family in great danger of a retaliation from the other people of surrounding cities; who all considered us as a murdering, cowardly and betraying household. From then on, we always had to watch our backs.

To cap it all up, our very large family of origin, dad's nuclear-extended polygamous family, started out with, and has always been plagued with betrayals, deceptions and in-fighting. Ours was like a circus act with wives always at one another's throats, and the children simply following suit, but took the in-fighting to greater heights. Part of which led to my brothers selling me off into slavery under the pretense that I must have been killed by a wild animal.

But here was dad now returning to a vibrant worshipful relationship with God as he visited Beersheba. God responded to him that night in Beersheba, when He spoke with dad in a dream of the night. God confirmed that it was His will and plan to relocate our dynasty to Egypt at this period in time to take care of us there.

God further told dad that he should not be afraid to go down into Egypt because his dynasty will become great there, and dad would later pass on from this life in Egypt under the watchful eyes and care of Joseph – and yes, Joseph truly is alive and the leader of Egypt as I had planned. But my plan to give you Canaan as your permanent inheritance has not changed with this relocation to Egypt – this is a temporary stop or move – because I will still return your dynasty back to Canaan when the time is right.

And with that visitation from God with daddy in his visions of the night, dad got up the next morning with a confirmed assurance that he was going in God's will and plan to the land of Egypt. In spite of what all the circumstances had earlier pointed to, it was most important for dad to clearly hear from God Himself on such a major decision and change as this.

The journey to Egypt was then resumed and all of dad's living wives, children and their wives, grandchildren, cattle and all the rest of their belongings made the trip to Egypt. Without counting the children's wives, the number of direct descendants of dad that made the trip to Egypt were seventy (70) in all.

Chapter 19

Closed Doors and Open Doors

Welcome to the New

As daddy and all the members of his large family walked away from the currently closed door of the land of Canaan and into the open door of the land of Egypt, dad sent Judah ahead of him to notify Joseph of his impending arrival, and to get further directions to the city called Goshen where Joseph had prepared for them.

I then had my chariot (Rolls-Royce Phantom) prepared to take me to meet with daddy and the rest of the large family as they were arriving in Goshen. When I set my eyes on my father again, words could not describe the waves upon waves of emotions that swept over myself and daddy and we grabbed onto each other as if whatever had caused our separation all these years might try to pull us apart again if we didn't hold on to each other tightly enough.

We hugged and sobbed and hugged some more, and then sobbed even more. This live meeting seemed so unreal and much more like a dream, because neither of us had ever expected to see each other alive again in this world. We had both lived in 'different worlds' over the past two decades with the thought of not even being sure whether either of us was alive.

We both looked over each other's faces and whole posture as if to determine if the person right in front of either of us was truly who each of us said we were. We wanted to be sure that neither of us was wearing a mask and that no one was playing any hanky-pinky games on us and our emotions. 'Joseph, is it truly you?' Dad asked in what seemed like uncountable number of times.

'It sure is really me, your precious long lost son; see my birth marks and know assuredly that it really is I'. I also whispered the special names I used to call him when it was only he and I that were playing together during my growing up years back at home him. I watched as his eyes lightened up with a spark of realization that this was truly me.

'Welcome to the new and to the land of Egypt, daddy. It is the land of our dreams that God had shown us decades ago in dreams and visions of the night, when we kept pondering what those dreams meant. But daddy, now that you're sure that it is truly I, please, let me know of a certain that this is truly you also; tell me the special things you used to say to me alone in my ears as I grew up'.

Dad then turned and whispered all the encouraging words he used to speak to me alone as a child. My eyes also lit up like the noon day sun shining in its brightest strength as he whispered the prayers he used to pray over me while I grew up under his protective arms. He used to prayerfully say that whenever I call for help from a person, multitudes will respond to me with more than the help I could imagine.

I used to wonder at what kind of prayers those were, as they really didn't make much sense to me back then. I wondered how a person could ever be offered more help than he requested for and also how multitudes will respond to a call to one person. Now it made much sense to me as it dawned on me that this prayers of my dad had been answered by God in God's own way and time.

Now I see how people from all over the world troop down to Egypt on a daily basis, in order to buy food from us. And with the multitude around offering the very best from their nations in exchange for food, it never ceases to amaze me when I speak to a person, how so many respond until I clarify who exactly I was referring to.

When several people from different nations would all respond at the same time to me at my request to a person to bring their best forward, I used to think it was simply because of the language differences between us, and the various people from different parts of the world. But I later realized that they all responded because they also needed what (the food) I could give them, and were paranoid as to whether if they are not attended to first, if there would still be any left-over food for them by the time it got to their normal turn.

Dad and I basked in each other's warm embrace and most like gave each other one tenth (1/10th) of a bath as we soaked and drenched each other in our tears of joy from the reality of a day that still feels like a dream but staunchly points to the all-knowing and all-powerful nature of the Most High God in fulfilling the indestructible dreams that he puts in our hearts.

After we sobered up enough from our tears of joy, dad then said that he is very grateful to the Most High for giving him the privilege to see and hold me in his arms again. He said he feels very fulfilled, happy, joyous and satisfied haven seen me alive again before his own death, that he now feels he can die now and depart out of his world in perfect peace and happiness.

But I told him 'nice try dad, but you are not going nowhere yet; you got a new life ahead of you filled with recapturing lost years that we have missed spending together, and my children also need time with you, their grandpa, whom they never met until now. I know you feel like you would like to 'check out while the ovation is loudest', or leave the world in all this joyous mood because you don't want any negative incidence to spoil it for you.

But, let me tell you something daddy, just as the Lord promised you newness, he also promised newness to me; and as it is written, 'what the Lord does abides forever'. We are not suffering anymore tragedies as that time has passed and God has also helped us to pass the necessary tests of life and to eventually come out victorious on the other side of it.

Newness, Progress and Provisions Require Peace to Thrive

I then addressed the entire family and welcomed them all. 'Welcome to the land of Egypt, God's prepared new home for you. God had gone ahead of us all to prepare this place to support and sustain our dynasty for as long as God deems fit, before returning us back to the promised land of Canaan.'

'As you all can see, God sent me ahead and promoted me to be the Prime Minister, Governor or Official Ruler (or whatever title works for you to call me by) over Egypt, in His own incredible ways and time. And it was the King of Egypt, the Pharaoh himself that God miraculously used to promote me'.

'The Pharaoh was the 'God' over Egypt before he had an encounter with the Almighty that not only revolutionized his own personal life, but mine, the people of Egypt, and as we have come to see what is presently being unfolded before all of our eyes, the world as a whole. The Pharaoh stepped down willingly from being referred to as 'God' to rest content in his title as the King of Egypt.'

'So the Pharaoh is the overall Ruler of Egypt and he made me his second in command to officially rule over the whole nation. I have learned a lot over the years about the likes and dislikes of the Egyptians just like each and every other race or ethnicity in the world have their own peculiar likes and dislikes'.

'I will guide you so that everyone who is new in Egypt will know how to wisely live among the people of Egypt, and how to relate with them, so that we do not become unnecessarily offensive to one another. One notable dislike of Egyptians is the smell of cattle rearing. Don't get me wrong, they love the meat of cattle when it has been prepared in delectable ways - barbecue, deep frying etc. - but want nothing to do with the raising of the cattle or the people that raise such.

'Don't be quick to judge them as being hypocritical in loving the prepared meat of cattle but wanting nothing to do with either the rearing of the cattle or even those that do such rearing; because I have found out that every race or group of people have their own peculiarities that may never make sense to people of other races or ethnicity. You all for example, consider it an abomination to completely shave off your hair or wear mascara (make-up), but these are norms for Egyptians.'

'As a matter of fact, Egyptians consider cattle rearing as well as the cattle keepers to be an abomination or a taboo for them to do anything in common with – even something as small as eating at the same table together. I will tell you to please respect their individuality and differences so that we can all live together in peace as this is God's will and plan for us over the next few years, decades or centuries.'

'I want to encourage us to be very wise in relating with and answering everyone in the land, beginning with the Pharaoh. I will soon visit the Pharaoh to announce your arrival and I will be letting him know that you are shepherds that raise livestock. That response to the Pharaoh will convince him to let you live in the land of Goshen – the outskirts of Egypt and the very best of the land'.

'Now, because Egyptian vehemently dislike the smell that comes from cattle rearing, they put cattle rearing far away from the major cities, and way off to the outskirts of the nation as a whole, in Goshen. But that has actually worked well for the city of Goshen, because it has been spared from all the industrial and residential pollution that is prevalent everywhere else.'

'Because Goshen is the place where all the cattle rearing in Egypt is done, it became a place that all

Egyptians avoided like a plague. It ironically has however become the very best part of Egypt. Goshen has been able to keep the natural, beautiful and breathtaking landscapes and clean air which is all but foreign to everywhere else in the nation'.

'You have all been cattle keepers most of your lives – I understand that some of you tried your hands at a few things here and there over time, like the 'whiz-kid' had a stint in the brokerage and financial investment world, but had moved back home to the cattle rearing business when the financial industrial crash happened'.

'I would therefore encourage you to put the cattle rearing first on your resume when the Pharaoh asks you about what you do. That way, he would naturally offer you the land of Goshen – the land of cattle rearing in Egypt – as a place for you all to settle down in and to naturally work out of. So, wisely and respectfully respond to the Pharaoh whenever he calls for you'.

Chapter 20

Silver Linings – Make the Best Out of the Worst Times

Perspectives and Rays of Hope

There will always be two sides to a coin, the head and the tail, just like there are two major times in each day, night time and day time, and also two major season of the cold time and the hot time; all representing two opposite sides to every situation or circumstance we will come across in life.

And many times, the circumstances and situations that get handed down to us or naturally surround us will be the supposedly 'negative', 'tail', 'nighttime of darkness'. But we have a choice of the perspective from which we choose to look at our situations from, and that will go a long way in either turning things all around for the best for us, or making it even worse than it started out as.

The Optimist and the Pessimist choose to look at the same glass that has water in it halfway from two different and opposite perspectives, which then determines what happens to either of them from that moment onwards. The Optimist chooses to see the glass as 'half-full', indicating he or she expects the water to keep going up in the glass - things to get better and better.

The Pessimist chooses to see the glass as 'half-empty', indicating he or she expects the water to keep going down in the glass until it is empty - for things to keep getting worse. And so each person's perspective or view point will determine what they do about their circumstance or situation; whether they make it better or worse.

This is why the Word of God encourages us to see things from the same view point of faith that God views things from, as opposed to the regular or natural view point of our sight or physical senses. This is why faith will work towards making things better, as opposed to worse because it believes the Word that says 'the path of the righteous will keep shining brighter and brighter until it becomes the best'; and 'all things are working together to produce good things for us because we love God and live in His purpose or will for us'.

I am telling you this because God has taken me through some of the most negative times of life -my brothers attempting to murder me and finally deciding to enrich themselves by selling me off into slavery for a much more grueling and slower death. I have gone through darkest nights of life in which I had to literally hold on to the only ray of hope or light available to me, which is the Word of God - while I was locked up in the darkest dungeons from an alleged crime that I never even attempted.

And even when the Lord lifted me from the dungeons of life and made me the Ruler over Egypt, such that I became the second richest and most powerful man on earth; yet I had never thought I would ever see any of my family of origin again in my lifetime. And that was why I named our first son Manasseh (God has made me forget all my hardships as well as all of my family of origin).

But God went beyond any of our wildest dreams, plans, wisdom, ambitions and machinations to prepare a place of reunion, nourishment, protection and comfort for all of our dynasty at a time when the rest of the world are going through one of the toughest and darkest times in history – a time of global famine and lack of productivity.

I pray for you today that God will give you rays of hope to hold on to in your darkest nights so that you do not give up, or throw in the towel on the dreams and aspirations He has put in your heart. I also pray that He will work all things – good and seemingly bad – out for your very best, quite beyond your wildest imaginations and hopes, just like He did for me, in Jesus mighty name.

Successful On-boarding through our Skills, Talents and Character

I then went on to see the Pharaoh to inform him of the arrival of my dad as well as his dynasty. To ensure that the visit went well and was void of overcrowding, I selected five of my brothers to go with me, as opposed to the whole family crowding into the palace. When we came before the Pharaoh, I presented my brothers to him as representing the rest of the dynasty.

I introduced my brothers to the Pharaoh and I am sure they were quite surprised when the first question the Pharaoh addressed to them was what I had prepared them for; 'What do you guys do for a living?' the Pharaoh asked them. So they towed the line of answer I had prepared them with, but they also wonderfully built on it with their own flare and uniqueness, without straying from the core of the guidelines.

'We your servants are shepherds, just like our ancestors have also been. We raise the healthiest and fattest cattle ever, using the most natural vegetation's for their food, and avoiding the use of chemical growth hormones that though appears to speed up the growth of the cattle, but really just leads to cancerous growths in everyone that later consumes such cattle.'

'And because we believe in giving the healthiest natural vegetation to the cattle we raise, we have brought all our cattle along from Canaan where there is no longer any healthy pasture to sustain them. We would humbly request for your favor and permission to live in the city of Goshen, where we learned that the cattle of this great land are raised.'

So the Pharaoh then turned to me and said that since my father and brothers have joined me here in Egypt, I should choose any place in the entire nation that I would want them to live in. He said he wants them to have the very best of Egypt and enjoy the blessings and goodness of the Most High God Who has used me tremendously to prepare Egypt for such a time as this.

He said he is sure that the land of Goshen will also be best for them since it has eventually become the best part of the nation, and since that is where all the cattle rearing takes place. He said they deserve the very best just as God has used me, from their dynasty to make Egypt the greatest nation on earth at this time – as the only source of food to the entire world.

The Pharaoh also asked me to put any of my brothers who possesses special cattle rearing skills in charge of his own personal livestock. This is where we also see that kings demand the very best of the best, and that they are always looking to better the best they have already achieved; as it is written, 'only the diligent will qualify to work for kings and in the highest places'.

And this is where we all must continually work in excellence; while never settling on the best we have achieved so far, but sharpening our skills, education and trainings, so as to make our best become merely good by the time we place it right next to what we have been able to improve on over time.

As the saying goes, 'good is the enemy of better, and better is the enemy of Best'. Our good skills, character, products and services, can and should always be improved on, rather than allowing it to become our resting or stopping points in life, our families, jobs, careers, communities, nations and most especially in our walk or relationship with the Almighty God.

The Meeting Place of the Secular and the Spiritual

It was now time for me to introduce my dad to the Pharaoh. And the wonderful thing about this meeting was the fact that it symbolized the meeting of the secular and the spiritual, the earthly and the heavenly, the giver and the receiver who quickly turn around and exchange roles so that the initial giver now becomes the receiver and the initial receiver now becomes the giver.

My father, Jacob, was representing the spiritual side because he had the Abrahamic covenant with the Most High God (God of Abraham, Isaac and now Jacob), in which God had promised to bless the whole world through his dynasty. The Pharaoh on the other hand, represented the secular or the earthly because he had the kingship of the most technologically advanced nation – essentially the greatest nation of our day on earth.

Each of the two sides had literarily believed that they practically had nothing in common and actually even considers the other side as an abomination before now. As I had earlier pointed out, our dynasty believed that we had the exclusive monopoly of relationships with God as seen from His relationship with our Patriarchs, which had made us believe that every other people were pagans or infidels or people who do not know the One true God, and would never know Him.

The Egyptians have always relied on their diligence, work ethics, skills, technological and military advancement; which had made them stand out as a world leader. They also had almost anything and everything needed, which seemed to have helped them in their advancement, one way or another. They worshipped the river Nile that supplied water and even worshipped some animals for various reasons.

To cap it all up, the Egyptians worshipped their king as the head of all the things that had 'given' them success; which is why they initially called and worshipped the Pharaoh as 'God' before He came face to face with the Most High God, when nobody and nothing could solve the dreams that troubled him back then.

This meeting that my father and I were heading to reminded me of that my meeting with the Pharaoh about ten years earlier. Only the Most High God could have arranged such a meeting and determined the outcome, as the outcome was way different from what any human being is capable of doing.

But the most important part of why God brings such meetings to happen, is to let both sides know, understand and come to terms or agreement with the fact that both sides are connected to Him in different ways and both sides are under His overall leadership. God also brings both sides to meet so that they can understand that the roles he gives them to play, will change at different times, and that no side is better than the other, or closer to God than the other.

Here was my dad, Jacob, representing the spiritual side, but having nothing to eat in the spiritual land of promise that God had promised to them, now coming to live under the roof or nation of the secular king of Egypt, the Pharaoh. And here was the Pharaoh whose nation's great successes and resources were not able to solve his dreams and dilemma about a decade ago.

God had however prepared me, a person of another race, perspective and beliefs, to serve as God's answer to him at that time, and now to be the bridge that brings both peoples and worlds together as one people, equally important and a blessing to one another, under the all-knowing and all-powerful benevolence and leadership of the Most High God. What an awesome God the Most High God is!

Who's your Daddy?

When we appeared before the Pharaoh, He asked my dad how old he was. And my dad replied that he had traveled this earth for one hundred and thirty years (130 years). Dad also told him that his life has however been filled with evil and short when compared to those of his ancestors. Let's look into the significance of their interactions so far.

The Pharaoh, as I had earlier said, was much older than I was, and maybe not quite as old as my dad, but I wouldn't say that there may have been too many years between both of their ages. But it was quite revealing when the first question he asked dad was about his age. I believe the reason for that question was the fact that dad seemed to have aged a whole lot more than his actual years.

That theory is supported by my dad's answer that his days really aren't that old but because they have been filled with evil that definitely have taken their toll on him, he does look far more advanced in years than he really is. Yet, my dad was supposed to be representing the spiritual side of life!

The question that the Pharaoh asked my dad could simply be rephrased as 'Who's your Daddy?' or 'Who has been directing the affairs of your life?' or 'To whom have you surrendered your life?' Now, it's quite telling also that the Pharaoh that was regarded as the secular, the mundane and the natural man, was the person asking dad, who was supposed to be regarded as the spiritual, the heavenly and the supernatural kind of man.

And everyone in the world would have to answer that question individually, as nobody else can answer it for another person. Everyone goes through different seasons in life, the dark times and the light times, productive and unproductive times, the valleys and the mountains etc.; but who we submit to and follow their lead is the one we can really call our daddy or leader.

Most people take full charge of their lives (which is good and commendable), but the only missing part is that they never submit to the leadership of the Almighty God. Most people are their own 'Gods' and would cheat, steal and kill to get their way in life, just like Satan, whom many supposedly spiritual or secular people would not want to admit to as being their 'daddy' or main influence.

And most people believe that we can escape or circumvent the God laid down principle of 'seed time and harvest', and 'Whatever a person sows is what they will reap – the fruit of the type of plant (thoughts, words or actions) a person sows is what he or she will harvest'. And the most painful part is that we allow the devil to deceive us with the lie that as God's 'special people', we somehow get preferential treatment and escape any negative harvest of what we've planted.

Just ask my dad to tell you his story [captured in detail in the book 'Who Am I? Going Rogue, by Dare Adebiyi (BenKing)], how he thought he had escaped away from the seeds of cheating others that he had planted before leaving home; only to get conned in a much bigger way from the person (people) he least expected it from.

Yet, dad has just gone through one of the happiest days of his life in not only hearing that I am alive after believing that I had died over twenty years ago, but to also find out that God had practically made me the richest and most powerful man in the world, putting me also in the position that I am able to feed, clothe and house all of his dynasty in the best comfort available in the world.

As if all that was not enough of a joy for dad, he and traveled based on the testimonial of his son's that

Joseph was truly alive and Ruler of Egypt, but he had met and seen me, and seen that everything that was as told to him, turned out to be true. But his happiest day had also turned to one of great sorrow as he had to confront the nagging question that gnawed away at his heart – what happened to Joseph decades ago when he went missing?

He had to deal with the greatest pain yet, which is to find out that his own ten (10) son's had *conned or deceived* him for over two decades in their 'fake' consoling him over the 'apparent death' of Joseph, while they were the actual cause of Joseph going missing. They had not only attempted to murder his 'special son', but they had actually sold him off into slavery forever [detailed in the book: Who Am I? Big Dreams by Dare Adebiyi (BenKing)].

Dad will very well confirm to you that this sayings of the Most High holds true, 'do to others what you would want others (not necessarily the same people you did yours to) to do to you', because 'it is want we plant or sow, that will come back to us in a harvest'. These forever settled Word or Principles of God should help guide us in how we treat other people on a daily basis.

But I hear you say 'what about forgiveness of sin's from God?' Forgiveness of sin primarily covers finding peace with God in and through Christ Jesus to ensure a place of living with Him forever in His Kingdom. Ask for the experience of dad even after his twin brother had forgiven him, his own son's then colluded to con him for over two decades.

Ask King David after he was told his sin were forgiven why the sword he had planted in killing an innocent man (Uriah), brought a harvest of untimely and unnecessary deaths to his family – Amnon, one of King David's sons raped his half-sister, Tamar, whose full brother, Absalom, later plotted revenge and killed Amnon, two (2) years later.

But that was before the work of salvation that Christ did for us all, you say; then ask the apostle Paul when he met Christ and He told him he was going to suffer much (persecution) for Christ (remember that persecuting the believers was his favorite pastime or hobby that he had sowed or planted for a while). Simply put, let's be conscious of what we do to others, because it has a nice way of coming back around in a much heavier dose.

Daddy then blessed Pharaoh (spoke words of blessings over him) before we left Pharaoh's presence, and of course, Pharaoh blessed (provided a place, and nourishment) daddy and all of his progeny also. At different times, God uses others to bless or give to us, at other times, He uses us to bless others. At any given time, He may use us to pronounce words of blessings, and at other times, to meet peoples physical needs (food, shelter, clothing); or the other way round.

No Wastage Permitted

My dad and all of his progeny went on to settle down in Goshen, the very best of the nation of Egypt. They had access to the best of buildings, amenities, security and nourishment. I sent each of the family households the nourishment needed according to how many people were in their household; nothing more, and nothing less.

It was very important that we adhere to God's savings lifestyle for us, as His way of providing for the days of no rain, no productivity or of famine. God is especially against wastage because for everyone that has more than enough, there is someone else out there who could make use of what others may consider as crumbs or leftovers that are usually wasted and not saved.

Some might have felt that they had come into such an abundance that they could never finish it in their lifetime, or even the lifetime of their children. And so feel that there is absolutely no reason to be saving, especially the leftover meals, because, as some might think, why preserve a meal you didn't finish when there will be a new and freshly made meal the next time you want to eat.

But I made everyone to understand that we must only eat so much and not too much, as if there is no tomorrow that will require food that we'll need to eat. I also brought everyone up to speed on the fact that it was as a result of following God's modus operandi of not consuming everything that comes in at a given season, that we are able to have some food saved for the opposite season when it shows up.

Now, this would have been the place to conclude my story; so, let's say this is where the cake has been baked and is done. We are however about to put the healthy icing on the cake. Let's talk about making some money, real cool money; of course, legally and while being a real blessing to others who are not as blessed or fortunate as us.

Chapter 21

Solving the Billionaire to Trillionaire's Simultaneous Equations (I)

Let's Make Some Money!

Yeah! Let's make some money! Moneys is good, and lots of it is also very good. Money can almost get us anything we want in this life. Money also confers great power, prestige, access, enjoyment and a host of other things on us when we have lots and lots of it. Which is why money is almost a number one thing that many people are willing to do just about anything for; and I mean 'anything', especially for a large sum of money.

It is said that 'money is the answer to everything' or that 'money gives everything'. But let's start off by qualifying that statement, because money can actually *only* answer to or give everything that money can buy, get or give - but truly not everything else. As much as money can actually get most things on this side of eternity or in the world, there are way more important things that money cannot buy, get or give.

Before we talk more about making lots and lots of money, let's get real with ourselves on two fundamental things about money. One, is that we should not allow money to dictate to us who we should be, how we should live or what to do with it - don't let money make us inhumane and a monster to others. Two is knowing what money can get and what it cannot get - let's touch on just a few that should drive the point home:

1. Money can buy you the biggest of houses and mansions (could turn out to be a place of great strife, betrayal, abuse, hostility and even death), but it cannot buy you a home (a refuge, shelter or place where you love, are loved and feel safe).
2. Money can buy you the most expensive of clothes, but if a person is paralyzed, he or she cannot dance around as they would have wanted in such clothing.
3. Money can attract almost anybody in the world to come and be with you, but it can never buy their true love, affection, loyalty or faithfulness.

4. Money can buy you the most delicious of meals, which is worthless to a person who is not able to eat, or tolerate that kind of food because of allergies, or whose taste buds are dead.
5. Money can buy you all the luxuries in the world, but cannot buy you happiness; which is why some of the richest people in the world end up committing suicide.
6. Money can buy you the best places on earth, even a seat at the table with kings and queens, but it cannot buy you a place in the kingdom of God whenever you leave this world - that was paid for by the sacrifice of Christ.

Simply put, don't let money become your 'God' such that you are controlled by it, especially in a negative way - like my older half-brothers allowed money to tell them to sell their teenage brother off into slavery back then. Be the master over money and not the servant of money. Also, use money positively as opposed to negatively or wickedly.

Money can be used positively in catering for our needs, those of the people closest to us, and even those who have no one directly related to them that can help meet their necessary needs. However, using money negatively is like anyone that believes they can buy a person and do just about anything evil they can think of to them. There are, unfortunately, a myriad of other terrible and unimaginable things that people can, and continue to concoct in cruelty against others.

Since we have gone over the basics about money, it advantages, uses and limitations, let's move on to the things and ways to help us make lots of money.

The Simultaneous equations of Receiving and Giving!

A big fundamental to making money is the willingness to receive money. We have to be intentional when it comes to making money. Making money cannot be left to chance or coincidence. And even though we will be using a lot of the money to help many people later on, it is first important for us to be intentional in receiving or making that money.

Money has to be in the right hands or the hands of people who will use the money to do good things and help others, especially those who are not able to help themselves at the particular given point in time. How do we know who will do good things with the money that comes to them and who will do wicked things?

Money and people are not the same, but they are very much related; they are like the two unknown variables (x and y) in a simultaneous equation. Each variable, though independent, is indirectly affected by what happens to the other variable; while what happens to that variable itself, also indirectly affects the other variable too. Some people will use money to help others in need, while others will use money to be cruel to others in need

God tests each and every one of us to show us what is in our hearts, and to show us both of our money and people management skills. And He starts off small, so that it is easier to pass the smaller tests before moving on to tougher ones. That's why He says that whoever is faithful in little, will be entrusted with more – meaning that whoever does good things with the little that initially comes to them will be entrusted with more.

There are days and times when we give to charities or give charitably, or when we use our monies, gifts, talents, time or resources to do things for others without requiring payment in return; but there are other times that we cannot, or must not give away our gifts, talents, skills, time or resources without receiving payment in return.

It is very crucial to receive payment at such times, because those are the times and instances that make money for us, out of which we can later on also do charitable things from. This also represent when the

Word talks about each one of us choosing not to steal but to rather do honest labor or work with our own hands, talents and abilities, that we will get paid for, and so have something that we are then able to share with others, or help others with.

We are encouraged by the Word of God not to be idle, nor be a burden to others in expecting their charity to eat, but to work or labor day and night so that we can pay for our needs and go on to helping others who cannot do so at that particular moment in time. This is the premise upon which the next few sections will be built on.

Don't Be Scared of Making Money!

Very importantly, when it comes to making money, we cannot be faint of heart or scared of getting paid for the work or service that we render or give to others. As long as we know we are providing an honest and good product or service, we must be bold to receive payment for it. That is why God also said in His Word that the laborer is worth his or her wages. Get paid for the services and products you provide to others, and pay whoever provides a thing or service to you.

It is a person who has allowed the wicked devil to be his or her influencer or parent, that likes to take from others forcefully or deceitfully, without paying them - like the devil deceived the first couple by lying to them in order to take away their ownership and ruler-ship over God's creation, which God had originally entrusted into their hands. Such kinds of deception are varied and carried out in almost uncountable ways, few of which are:

Bribery, swindling, cheating, stealing with or without force or arms, raping, lying, betrayal, saying you'll pay later when you never intend to, enslaving others and forcing them to work without pay or deceiving oneself that he or she paid someone else for that 'slave' - because each person is supposed to be paid for what they do for you, and not for you to pay someone else, while leaving the laborer destitute.

Don't be scared of Giving Money Away!

The other side of the coin of moving from little to much or from the equations of the billionaire to that of the Trillionaire is the side of giving. The fear that challenges our natural mind or thinking is that 'how can we ever move from little to much, billionaire to trillionaire, if we give away the little that has come to us, earned from work or business, or received from trading, ventures or investments?'.

You may also ask, 'are we not supposed to save what comes to us to get it increased and especially for future times of lack of productivity or famine?' And, 'aren't we supposed to not be scared to get paid for anything we are also giving out?' These questions are very valid and we will look at what God has to say about them, as well as what some of the richest people in the world today do with their monies.

1. There is a time for everything on earth (under heaven) - a time to receive and a time to give. We must find the appropriate time for each of these two opposite activities; not confuse one for the other, and actually carry out the appropriate activity for each time.

2. The person who withholds or saves more than is good or appropriate for him or her, will soon become poor. Saving too much or inappropriately simply is when there's is no commensurate giving or outflow of what is being saved, but only the greed of hoarding.

3. Give, and it will be given back to us in the same percentage we have given out. Illustrated by the woman who gave 100% of what she had (2 coins), being referred to by Christ as having given the most (highest percentage of her money) that day

because those that gave way more money than she did, gave less than one hundred percent (<100%) of all they had, and not everything they had.

4. Anyone who gives to the poor is lending to the Most High God, Who promises to repay such givers well; and anyone who turns their eyes and hearts away from helping the poor will attract many curses to themselves.

5. Because God Himself is a Giver as seen in the scripture that says 'God so much loved the people of the world (His creations), that He gave up His only Son to become the sacrifice for their salvation, so that anyone who believes in Christ will not eternally perish but have the everlasting life from God.

6. And finally, is the saying of Christ Himself, which was not recorded in any of the gospels except in the book of Acts, that 'it is more blessed to give than to receive'.

Some of the Richest People in the World give over half of their Wealth Away, and get Richer!

Bill Gates and Warren Buffet are two people who have at one point or the other held the title of the World's

Richest Man alive. Bill Gates was named World's Richest Man for 13 consecutive years until 2008 when Warren Buffet took that title for a period. But Warren Buffet soon gave away almost half of his billions – a move that intentionally relinquished that 'coveted' title of the 'Richest Man in the World'.

Buffet then went on to lead other billionaires to commit to what he, Bill and Melinda Gates, and Mark Zuckerberg called 'The Giving Pledge' in 2009. It is a pledge available only to Billionaires, in which each billionaire that chooses to join will commit to giving over 50% of their wealth to charitable efforts over the course of their lifetime or in their 'will' for after they leave this world.

Buffet shows that the principle of giving to receive, laid down by God is real, valid and dependable. After giving out almost half of his wealth in 2008, and being left with just $37 billion, Buffet has been blessed in return and has more than doubled his wealth ten (10) years later. Today, Warren Buffet is worth US$82.9 billion

It is true that the children of this world are wiser than the children of light; and the first will become the last, while the last will become the first. Those considered people of this world follow the principles of giving and receiving what is commensurable in return. Don't complain that the rich keep getting richer because they follow God's principles of getting richer by giving stupendously.

Warren Buffet has committed to giving away 99% of his wealth while Bill and Melinda Gates have committed to giving away 95% of their wealth. As of today, there are almost 200 Billionaires who have joined The Giving Pledge from different walks of life and businesses – Pizza, hair care, technology, home improvement, social media etc. And their combined pledges so far is close to US$1 trillion that they are giving away for the betterment of the world.

If you want to join the club of the richest people in the world, start out from where you are today by being a generous giver, especially to those who are not able to care for themselves or their loved ones, and to charitable causes or godly causes. When God see's your heart and consistency, He will move you higher and higher and you will soon be able to join the 'Giving Pledge' with me.

Chapter 22

Solving the Billionaire to Trillionaire's Simultaneous Equations (II)

Different Ways of Paying for Food

And so grain or food became even more and more scarce in Egypt and other nations of the world as the years of famine progressed without any food growing across the globe. Soon, people in the land ran out of any forms of food to buy or sell to others. They then sought out to buy food from the several national sites where we had stored and preserved foods from the years of plenty or great productivity.

I asked my assistants to open up the storehouses and begin to sell grain and food to the people of Egypt also. At very low prices, food was being sold to every

Egyptian, and International that came to buy food. I however, received all the payments in the name of, and for my king, the Pharaoh.

Soon, Egypt got to the place in time where money simply was no longer available to the people to buy more food with – people simply ran out of money. But the famine and lack of productivity was not yet over; so *the people came to me, still requesting for help and for food.* Do take note that it was the people that came up to me requesting for my help on what they could do to survive the famine.

They needed food but no longer had money to pay for it, even though it was really cheap. So I told them that they could use other things apart from money to pay for the food. I pointed out that they could use their livestock's – horses, cattle and other animals – to make payments. This seemed very welcoming to them as 'according to their own words 'it is better for us to give our livestock's instead of dying of starvation'.

For the rest of that particular year of continuous famine, the people brought in their livestock's to pay for food. That way, they and their families were able to buy food for themselves and outlast the famine of that particular year. But as the year was approaching it's end, so also were the people gradually running out of livestock's to trade with. With the livestock's traded in,

I had also gathered all such livestock's in the name of, and for my king, the Pharaoh.

Let Your Creativity Loose!

In order to make lots of money, we must be willing to be creative - see possibilities beyond what is immediately obvious or available - and really let our creative minds loose. Just looking around will inspire you at what others have been able to dream of, and gone on to create. Look at all the different hairstyles that barbers and hair stylists have come up with; the different architectural designs on buildings ; different models of cars, jets, boats, cruise liners, electronics, phones, watches etc. and people are still crying for more and more.

Imagine the number of songs out there, yet new songs are still being composed, sung and still become billboard hits; countless movies out there, yet new ones are still being made that outsell the most successful ones before; numerous books beings written, yet new ones still become New York Times Bestsellers, Amazon Best sellers and worldwide best sellers like this book will soon be.

Don't let people and your circumstances or environment continue to lie to you that you are a nobody and that you cannot be successful with your flare, inclinations, designs, productions, services, books, movies, food, styles, music, instrumentation's, packaging, talk, inventions etc. What may look meaningless to some people, will mean the world to others - move away from the negative people and find those who will celebrate what you have to offer.

We must also be willing to spot opportunities where others see no way, nothing special, or they just do not want to do that particular thing. For example, the people of Egypt had grains, but were looking for bread - for someone to bake the grains into bread. They had cattle, but were not willing to prepare it into mouth-watering steak - rare, medium-well or well-done.

I took up all what they didn't want to have to do - rearing cattle, living close to cattle, cleaning cattle up and cutting it up into premium cuts like the T-bone and sirloin cuts, threshing grains and cleaning out the dirt in it, before grinding it and baking it into hot buttery succulent loaves of white, wheat, sourdough, or multi-grain bread; and of course got paid for taking on such ventures.

Simply put, what others are unwilling to take on or to do because they consider it as useless, or a waste of their time and energy, demeaning or below their status in life, may be your own ticket to making big bucks or money out it. Find what you love to do or have a passion for; or what you believe should be improved on, and then go ahead to improve on it, or recruit those that will do it for you.

Pay attention to what you consider missing or lacking in a place, thing or experience, and see how you can proffer a solution, invention, product or service that solves the issue at hand. For example, a man with a sizable head found out that no sunglasses on the market were big enough for his head, and so went about starting a very successful company making extra-large sunglasses for people like him - a very large number of people.

Bill Gates found that computers can become a staple of all people all over the world, if only such computers were made to be very easy to use and intuitive to the least learned or educated person. He then went on to create the windows operating system that took a lot of the mystery out of using computers for the average layman or worker. That soon made him the world's richest man for several years until even the government officials became so envious of him that they started attacking him with all kinds of new regulations.

What are you going to do, sing, draw, write, produce, record, compute, code, color, create, fashion, mesh together, teach, take on, erase, add on, multiply, correct, enforce, advocate, get paid for, give, stitch, sow, mend, carry out, collect, sell, buy, buy and resell at a profit, trash, combust, synergize, empower, save, renew, restock, repeat, recreate, resource, rescind, report, repackage, retry, respect, research, restructure, reengineer, remodel, revamp etc. that will make good money for you as you enjoy and bask in what you do?

The world is waiting for you; now get up to doing that thing stupendously well, and you will soon know what it is to be very successful and rich!

The Science that Restored the Land; the Taxes that Grew the Economy

Finally, the people came around to me again when they ran out of food with the proposal to exchange their lands and labor for food. In their very own words, the people requested to not only give their lands to the Pharaoh in exchange for food, but they also asked to become servants to the Pharaoh so that he becomes permanently responsible for their upkeep and they wouldn't have to come back for help every time they were out of food.

I took their proposals and worked something agreeable with it and out of it. If the king and the leadership of the nation was encouraged to be responsible for the upkeep of the people, especially in such trying times as this, then the people would need to contribute what they can to make that happen.

I set up agreements so that both the people and the leadership (the king and his officials) would work together and use the power of oneness and synergy to produce astronomical or geometrical growth in the economy, and an enduring legacy of one nation under God at all times – times of good or bad, plenty or famine, success or failure.

As the people had proposed, deeds were written for the sale of the lands to the king in exchange for food being made available regularly to the people for their survival and upkeep. Also, I would be making the technology and science of fertilization and irrigation available to the people so that they could make the grounds productive again.

In return, the people were to move to cities that the soil tests had shown were least damaged and were quickest to respond to fertilization so that they could start growing agricultural produce again; as we have been able to successfully do in the city of Goshen. Oh, did I forget to tell you that we had been able to get the ground in Goshen back to a productive state?

Yeah, that's our best kept secret, and one of the reasons why we were able to say that Goshen had become the best part of Egypt by the time my family of origin arrived to stay. That's also why we had been able to start rearing cattle there again. God had helped us to discover how to fertilize the ground and put back all the lost nutrients it needed to start growing grass and crops again.

When God had interpreted the dreams He gave to the Pharaoh over ten years earlier, we had thought that we got all of the interpretation back then before the seven (7) years of plenty even showed up, followed by the seven (7) years of famine. But as time went forward, Got released more interpretation to us as the years of the famine was moving into its second (2nd) year.

God had revealed to us that the feces, poop or dung of the livestock were a good means of restoring the lost nutrients in the soil of the farms. He explained to us that the reason the first dream was about livestock while the second dream was about ears (vegetation) was because the waste produce of the livestock holds the key to restoring the lost nutrients of the farmlands, which became the challenge of the seven years of famine

The livestock feces emanated very heavy stench or smell, which naturally put many people off who just couldn't stand a bad smell. This was especially true of the Egyptians born in the land, which may be one of the reasons why they considered those that had a passion or flare for rearing cattle as weird, or as an aberration – the abnormal.

Funny thing is that everyone passes out farts (gas) and other liquid or solid wastes (urine, poop, or feces) that stink, but that doesn't make us dislike or regard ourselves as weird or an abomination. And even funnier is the fact that my fellow Egyptians loved their meats a lot (of course that's when it's already made into the rare, medium rare or well done steak they relish), but they just act like the barbecued livestock they consume had no history of being raised in a stinking environment - which is why they pay big bucks ($) to those willing to prepare their 'juicy' steaks.

I also made agreements that the people would be given seeds to plant in the lands and to nurture them to maturity and harvest. They were then to give back one fifth of their harvests to the Pharaoh for savings against such natural disasters as the famine we were experiencing, and for use to grow the economy to further heights. I then proceeded to give the people seeds to plant in the farm lands and to cultivate such unto fruition.

That was how the Lord God Almighty made the nation of Egypt into the World's most successful and formidable nation of our time; and how He also made me into a trillionaire handling the affairs to the only nation He had chosen to not only survive the famine, but to also help other nations to survive the same.

When I look back over the journey that the Most High God had taken me through, I cannot but worship Him in awe and holy reverence. He truly not only knows the future from the beginning, but also holds that future in the palm of His Hands. I stand in amazement of His showing me His indestructible dreams and plans from when I was a teenager; and though the enemy did his worst to destroy that dream, the Almighty came victoriously through for all of us.

<u>Conclusion</u>

I dare and challenge you to submit (entrust, commit) yourself into the able and everlasting arms of the Most High God, through faith in His Son, Jesus Christ; and always lean-on His Spirit to help you walk through your short journey on earth, through to His everlasting Kingdom.

I commit you into the mighty Hands of the Most High God, the Creator of the Heavens and Earth, the all wise and all-knowing God, the only One who reveals the end from the beginning, and allows the enemy of our lives (Satan and those that intentionally or not, submit to his influences and leadership), to do his very worst against us, only to find out that his worst has been used by God to bless us and take us to His very best for us.

Do also remember these pertinent principles to help guide your everyday choices and decisions:

1. Let God be the One Who tells you Who You Are! Don't let the Devil, or those that he works through – unbelieving or ungodly relatives (parents, uncles, aunties, cousins, grandparents, favoritism-playing parents), satanic inspired prophets or future tellers, envious and murderous siblings (brothers and sisters), those in the places of one form of authority or another who refuse to acknowledge God in their work or practice (doctors, midwives, nurses, teachers, pastors, ministry leaders, bosses, subordinates, Presidents, Governors, Senators, Representatives, CEO's, Law makers, Judges, Attorneys, Financial professionals etc.; be the ones that define you.

2. There is no escaping of the harvests of whatever we sow or plant either in our own lives or the lives of others. It may takes several years of germination and growth, and most of the times, we would have forgotten about what we did, said, or refused to do or say; but the harvest will definitely arrive someday. So, plant wisely every day! Do to others, what you would want others to do to you or to your generations to come.

3. There is nobody that God cannot use for us, just like He used an 'unbelieving King or Pharaoh' to pull me out of the dungeons of life, and to put me in the most prestigious and influential position ever.

4. There is also nobody that the devil cannot infiltrate to use against us and God's dreams for our lives, just like he used my dad to play the favoritism game, and my siblings to play the envy game. So be very prayerful and watchful so as not to play into the hands of currently satanic infested people who act as if they are looking out for your good.

5. Trust in the Lord with all of your heart and never lean on your own understanding or prowess; commit your life and moments to Him and He will direct and order your life in the very best way.

6. Forgive those that do wrong things against you, so that God can also forgive you your own wrongs against others. We all want God and others to forgive us of *all* our wrongs, so let's extend the same forgiveness to *all* other people too.

7. Moving with the wise will make you wiser, while moving with fools will make a person more foolish.

8. Dare to be different for God and for what is right.

9. God already has great and good plans for you, don't lose out on it by thinking you're smarter than Him.

10. Work hard and smart to be the top or head at whatever you do.

11. Never say never about the great dreams and ambitions that God has put in your heart.

12. Always save aggressively for the days or years of lack of productivity.

13. Leave vengeance to God to handle, so that you don't get in His way when He starts repaying someone for their wickedness.

14. Let the enemy do their very worst, as they will eventually come to terms with the fact that they were still working for God to fulfill His purposes and plans.

15. Whatever the circumstances and situations that surround you, God will exceed your wildest dreams and imaginations in Jesus.

Thank you for taking the time to buy and read this life and destiny empowering book. Get the other best-selling books of Dare Adebiyi (Oludare Adebiyi), and get them for everyone you know, and you would want to see become the very best that God has prepared for them to be!

About the Author

Dare Adebiyi is the Bestselling author and producer of the 'Who Am I?' Series, which sold out in minutes at its inaugural launch; and is in the making of over 1,000 other titles – including this 'The Big Boss' Series.

He holds an MBA from Texas Southern University, worked in Management at different firms and held the FINRA Series 7 (General Securities Rep/Financial Advisor), NASAA Series 66 (Uniform Combined State Law for Investment Advisers), TDI TX-5 (Life, Accident and Health Insurance), NMLS (Mortgage) and Underwriting Finder (Bonds) Licenses as a Financial Advisor at Morgan Stanley.

He is a strong proponent of Social Responsibility and giving back to the society. His team won the Regional Graduate School Business Plan Competition and went on to become National Finalists during his MBA Program. He is one of the regular Judges at the International Sustainable World Energy, Engineering, and Environmental Project (I-SWEEP) (USA) over several years. He is a regular Judge at the STEM Competitions of Harmony Public Schools.

He served on the Advisory Board of the Harmony Public Schools (the 2nd largest Charter School System in the United States), as well as the Advisory Board of

Hodges Bend Middle School, Houston Texas. He was the PTO President of the Sugar Land Harmony Science Academy (as it rose to become the Nation's topmost performing campus in the Harmony Public School System), and has won the Prestigious Star Parent Award for two (2) consecutive years (2015/16 and 2016/17). He also led the training department of Dominion (DCH, Houston) for several years, published the 'Leaders in Training' manual, and graduated many outstanding leaders from there.

He wears different hats at different times: CEO, Writer, Producer, Financial Professional, Trainer, Speaker and Life-Coach. He is a big believer in the incredible, the supernatural, the unfathomable, the paranormal, and the miraculous that he has been privileged to encounter severally. He and his lovely wife, Abi are blessed with two outstanding young men, Caleb and Enoch.

Notes

__*Notes*__

www.ingramcontent.com/pod-product-compliance
Lightning Source LLC
Chambersburg PA
CBHW070324220526
45467CB00001B/28